CORNWALL

Compact Guide: Cornwall is the ultimate quick-reference guide to this popular destination. It tells you all you need to know about the county: picturesque fishing villages, stunning beaches, the best waves for surfing, the profusion of exotic gardens and the futuristic Eden Project.

This is one of 133 Compact Guides, combining the interests and enthusiasms of two of the world's best-known information providers: Insight Guides, whose innovative titles have set the standard for visual travel guides since 1970, and Discovery Channel, the world's premier source of nonfiction television programming.

D1337330

Part of the Langenscheidt Publishing Group

Insight Compact Guide: Cornwall

Written by: Roland Collins
Updated by: Pam Barrett
Photography: Mark Read, Bill Wassman, Phil Wood
Additional photography: Pam Barrett 24/2, 33, 34; David Beatty, Bettman/Corbis 80/2; Hulton-Deutsch/Corbis 81, 83; Tony Halliday; Cornish Tourist Board/ David Hastilow; Mark Norton; Dawn Runnals; National Maritime Museum Cornwall/Bob Berry 40/2; Rick Stein 68; Trebah Garden Trust 42
Cover picture: Pictures Colour Library
Picture Editor: Hilary Genin
Maps: Apa Publications

Editorial Director: Brian Bell
Managing Editor: Maria Lord

CONTACTING THE EDITORS: As every effort is made to provide accurate information in this publication, we would appreciate it if readers would call our attention to any errors and omissions by contacting:
Apa Publications, PO Box 7910, London SE1 1WE, England.
Fax: (44 20) 7403 0290
e-mail: insight@apaguide.co.uk

Information has been obtained from sources believed to be reliable, but its accuracy and completeness, and the opinions based thereon, are not guaranteed.

© 2008 Apa Publications GmbH & Co. Verlag KG Singapore Branch, Singapore.

First Edition 1996; Second Edition 2002; Updated 2005; Revised 2008
Printed in Singapore by Insight Print Services (Pte) Ltd

Map of Truro based upon cartography supplied by
Estate Publications, licence no. 100019031

Worldwide distribution enquiries:
Apa Publications GmbH & Co. Verlag KG (Singapore Branch)
38 Joo Koon Road, Singapore 628990
Tel: (65) 6865-1600, fax: (65) 6861-6438

Distributed in the UK & Ireland by:
GeoCenter International Ltd
The Viables Centre, Harrow Way, Basingstoke,
Hampshire RG22 4BJ
Tel: (44 1256) 817-987, fax: (44 1256) 817-988

Distributed in the United States by:
Langenscheidt Publishers, Inc.
36–36 33rd Street 4th Floor, Long Island City, NY 11106
Tel: (1 718) 784-0055, Fax: (1 718) 784-0640

www.insightguides.com

Introduction

Top Ten Sights 4
Legend and Reality 7
Historical Highlights..14

Places

1: Saltash to Mount Edgcumbe....................................18
2: South Coast Harbours...23
3: Bodmin to Mevagissey 29
4: Truro to Falmouth..36
5: Helford to the Lizard 42
6: Land's End Peninsula 47
7: The Isles of Scilly 54
8: Art and Industry: St Ives to Camborne....................58
9: The North Coast Resorts 64
10: The Atlantic Highway 69

Culture

Painting and Sculpture...77
Architecture and Design 79
Literary Cornwall 80
Festivals 82
Music and Theatre 83

Practical Information

Food and Drink 85
Active Holidays 88
Practical Information 90
Accommodation..94

Index 96

◁ **Minack Theatre (p52)** A performance in this clifftop auditorium is a memorable experience.

▷**Fowey (p26)** The historic village and harbour have been an inspiration for novelists.

▷**Cotehele House (p19)** This historic house has beautiful gardens by the River Tamar.

◁ **St Michael's Mount (p49)** St Michael's Mount, accessible only by water at high tide, has a rich history as well as a dramatic situation.

◁ **The Eden Project (p33)** The Eden Project, in a disused quarry near St Austell, has proved a huge success, attracting millions of visitors each year to explore the vegetation in the vast biomes of this gobal garden.

△Tintagel (p73)
Arthur's legendary castle, set on a sheer, windswept headland, retains some of its mystic charm.

◁ **Polperro (p25)**
One of the prettiest fishing villages in Cornwall, Polperro bans cars from the narrow streets that run down to the tiny harbour, reducing pollution and preserving its old-world atmosphere.

◁ **Surfing (p88)**
Cornwall's Atlantic beaches have exhilarating waves for surfing.

▽**Tresco Gardens
(p56)** The mild climate of the Scilly Isles allows exotic plants to flourish.

◁ **Tate St Ives (p59)**
The quality of the light in St Ives has been attracting artists since the 19th century. Now, Tate St Ives, on Porthmeor Beach, offers a stunning setting for works inspired by or connected with Cornwall.

Cornwall – Legend and Reality

Cornwall offers the best of all worlds. Cross the River Tamar from Devon and you find yourself in another land, mysterious and magical, almost Mediterranean in places, yet reassuringly British in its customs, currency and language (although the Cornish place names are exotically different).

This is a place of legend and fantasy, the land of King Arthur, of pixies, smugglers, pirates, wreckers and saints, all of it underpinned by the haunting relics of even more mysterious and ancient cultures. On Cornwall's misty moorland and along its rocky coast, prehistoric stone circles and burial chambers, cliff castles and hill forts punctuate the landscape.

They are interspersed with the gaunt ruins of mine stacks and engine houses, symbols of the county's once vigorous tin and copper mining industries. More evident still, of course, is the real Cornwall of today, enriched by its people who maintain strength and forbearance in the face of harsh economic realities. They are the most friendly and welcoming of hosts.

SEAGOING HERITAGE

Cornwall's seagoing past is vital to its identity. Along 300 miles (482 km) of varied coastline the spirit of the old 'free traders', as they were euphemistically called, is enshrined in the names of hidden coves, secret tunnels and caverns and in the history of wonderful old inns. Colourful memories of smuggling and piracy apart, Cornwall's beleaguered yet still active fishing industry fascinates the visitor at bustling harbours such as Newlyn, Mevagissey and Looe, and the county's noble tradition of lifesaving is enshrined in lifeboat houses and coastguard lookouts.

TREASURES

Cornwall is lavish with its treasures: the golden beaches and azure seas

Rejected by Rome

It seems that the Romans couldn't be bothered with Cornwall. This rugged, sea-lashed peninsula lay well beyond their main lines of communication and, apart from a few minor dwellings and guard posts, they did not settle in the far west. For Cornwall's Iron Age people, the so-called Celts, life went on much as it always had. Cornwall therefore lacks the Roman remains that can be found in many other parts of Britain.

Opposite: surfing at Newquay
Below: Tate St Ives exhibit

of the Land's End Peninsula; the wooded sea inlets of Helford Creek and the River Fal; towering cliffs like Pentire on the north coast; handsome churches such as Launceston's St Mary Magdalene with its sculptured granite walls; Truro's Georgian townscape; Norman castles like Restormel, and country houses such as Tudor Cotehele on the River Tamar.

Adding zest to all this are colourful festivals such as Padstow's 'Obby Oss' celebration on 1 May, Helston's Flora Day a week later, and Penzance's Mazey Day in June. In recent years Cornish cuisine has come into its own, with imaginative use of the county's rich natural produce from land and, especially, sea. Cornwall is the home of marvellous pottery and great art, as the Tate St Ives Gallery proves, with its celebration of some of Britain's most famous modernist painters at the heart of an atmospheric fishing village, above sparkling surf and golden sands – Cornwall encapsulated.

FORMATION OF THE LAND

The geological formation of Cornwall's spectacular coastline is a fascinating subject. The white feldspar, grey quartz and black mica found in some of the granite is typical of igneous rocks formed when magma (molten rock) cooled and

Below: the Cornish are proud of their maritime tradition
Bottom: Widemouth Bay, near Newquay

crystallised. Some of the granite quarried near Penryn is 290 million years old. The slate that is so typical of Cornwall is a metamorphic rock that has been changed from the original sedimentary mudstone by enormous pressures and temperature changes. Black slate is rich in silica, derived from the shells of tiny animals.

EARLY CIVILISATIONS

Cornwall's ancient peoples have left a dramatic mark on the landscape. The Neolithic, Bronze Age and Iron Age tribes of the far west used resilient granite in their sacred monuments and buildings. In spite of pillaging by Victorian 'antiquarians' many of Cornwall's ancient monuments survive in some form. They make the far west of the county, especially, one of the richest archaeological treasure houses in Europe. Famous features include the Neolithic quoits or dolmens, huge granite uprights supporting an enormous slab. These structures once formed the core chamber of earthen burial mounds. The finest examples include Trethevy Quoit on Bodmin Moor, Zennor Quoit and Mulfra Quoit on the lonely hills of the Land's End peninsula, and the roadside Lanyon Quoit on the moors above Penzance.

From the later Bronze Age period date the dramatic stone circles of Bodmin Moor and the Land's End peninsula. The Bronze Age people developed metal working. They settled in farmsteads and buried their dead in tumuli, small stone cysts covered with earth.

IRON AGE

By approximately 100BC, bronze gave way to iron, and the great works of the Iron Age can be seen in the remains of defensive walls that were thrown across spectacular headlands to create impregnable promontory forts and trading centres. These 'cliff castles' are at their most dramatic at Tintagel and The Rumps on the North Cornish coast, and at Gurnard's Head and Logan Rock (Treryn Dinas) in the far west. Some of the most impressive

Stone circles
A Christian culture unable to explain the purpose of the ceremonial sites on the Moor and the Land's End peninsula gave them fanciful names. Several stone circles are known as 'The Merry Maidens', reflecting a mythical tale of girls being turned to stone for daring to dance on the Sabbath.

Bodmin Moor, untamed and dramatic

remains are at Carn Euny and Chysauster, both near Penzance, where the foundations and low walls of entire Iron Age villages have been beautifully preserved, the latter by English Heritage (tel: 07831-757934 for visits). They were still occupied in the 3rd century AD, indicating that Cornish society was already forming into a village network.

Below: Celtic cross
Bottom: a timeless scene –
moonlight over the water

GOD AND MAMON

The 4th century AD, the end of the so-called Dark Ages, was illuminated by Celtic Christianity, with the arrival of missionaries from Ireland and Wales. Many of them were also shrewd traders. Cornwall was a stop on the sea route from Ireland and South Wales to Brittany, and merchants, missionaries and pilgrims would disembark at Padstow on the north coast. From there they followed a route across country to Fowey on the south coast where they would take ship once more – a better bet than risking the often deadly sea passage round the awesome Land's End, known from ancient times as Belerion, the 'Seat of Storms'.

THE CELTS AND KING ARTHUR

Religion went hand in hand with superstition, and the long established myths of pre-Christian times grew. The saints were said to have magical powers.

Heaven and Hell came to earth in the form of princesses, mermaids, fairies, giants, pixies and monsters. King Arthur emerged as the Cornish champion against the barbarian Saxon invaders. Tintagel, the Iron Age Celtic settlement, seems dramatically well suited to being the royal seat and scene of Arthur's exploits. Although a large question mark hangs over its history, the modern 'Arthurian industry' flourishes and Tintagel is one of Cornwall's busiest tourist resorts.

INVASION AND REBELLION

The Saxon invasion, and the Norman one that followed, left some mark on Cornwall. Norman influence is expressed mainly in numerous churches with characteristic square towers. Cornwall's innate individualism and rebelliousness remained strong. The county took up arms against Henry VIII's taxes and, in 1549, against the imposition of Protestantism. The most divisive event was the Civil War (1642–46) when many battles were fought in the west.

POPULATION, LANGUAGE, RELIGION

The River Tamar, rising only 4 miles (6 km) from the north coast, made Cornwall's peninsula into a virtual island with its own language and customs. The language belongs to the same linguistic group as Welsh and Breton. It was in everyday use in Cornwall for many centuries but ceased to be a living language in the late 18th century. It is being revived today by enthusiasts, and can be learned in evening classes, but for visitors it survives most vividly in the numerous place names that add to Cornwall's romantic character.

Neither the Romans nor the Anglo Saxons made much impact on Cornwall and, in spite of the erosion of their distinctive language, the Cornish retained a strong individuality that is still apparent today. Added to this is a deeply religious instinct that the 18th-century evangelist John Wesley channelled into Methodism, still a strong element of Cornish life. Hand in hand with religion

End of the language
Cornish ceased to be a living language in 1777 with the death of a Mousehole fishwife, Dolly Pentreath, said to be the last person to converse in both Cornish and English. There is a monument to her in Paul churchyard, nearby.

Painted cottage doors in a Cornish village

goes a richness of imagination that has seen the Cornish encourage the colourful myths and legends that embroider their culture.

A CLEMENT CLIMATE

Cornwall has a remarkably diverse climate. The north and west coasts of the peninsula face the Atlantic and its bracing winds. The south and southwest coasts are sunnier and warmer. There are windless, winter days of clear blue skies and brilliant sun that remind you of high summer and compensate for the ferocious but exhilarating Atlantic gales – although high seas and global climate change are threatening these coasts in places (*see page 45*) and a fierce storm caused a devasting flood in Boscastle in August 2004. Spring comes early to the far west, when the cliffs are swathed in brilliantly coloured wild flowers, and autumn lingers late into the year. This fruitfulness is displayed in the county's many famous gardens, such as Glendurgan and Trebah on the banks of the Helford River, and Trelissick on the River Fal.

ECONOMY, TOURISM, ENVIRONMENT

Cornwall's remote situation creates economic difficulties. The old Cornish industries have been in decline for many years. Tin and copper mining

Below: blackberries in a hedgerow
Bottom: the remains of tin mines dot the countryside

are no longer viable, in spite of a conviction that Cornwall still holds vast mineral wealth in deep deposits. Of the old extractive industries, only a limited form of china clay and quarrying survive.

Cornwall's other great traditional industry, fishing, is struggling to maintain its viability. Diminishing fish stocks and EU regulations aimed at conserving them have led to the contraction of an already declining industry. As with fishing, so with farming; tastes change and an increasingly health-conscious public demands greater diversity and more regulated standards of production.

Economic regeneration and innovation in Cornwall's industry and commerce are essential if the county is to survive as more than a huge theme park. Yet tourism plays a major part in Cornwall's economic future. Greater personal mobility and an improved network of roads have made every part of the county more accessible. The Eden Project and the National Maritime Museum in Falmouth have attracted huge numbers of visitors and generated a lot of income. But environmental awareness focuses on the major dilemma: how to preserve the county's outstanding natural beauty while expanding tourism, which is necessary for economic survival.

The Minack Theatre offers culture in a stunning setting

KEEPING THE BALANCE

The balance between conservation and development is delicate, but, as elsewhere in Britain, there are a number of agencies and organisations working hard to preserve the best of the county's natural beauty and traditions. The National Trust's Enterprise Neptune scheme secured many miles of Cornish coastline that would otherwise have become privately owned, and the Trust was awarded the South West Coast Path Award in 2003. English Heritage, English Nature, and the RSPB also play a crucial part in preserving the best of Cornwall's archaeological and wildlife sites.

There are also many smaller agencies and local groups that guard and preserve the heritage of this extraordinary landscape. Further details can be obtained by visiting www.wildlifetrust.org.uk/cornwall.

HISTORICAL HIGHLIGHTS

40,000 BC *Homo sapiens sapiens* arrives in the peninsula.

10,000 BC Settlements begin around the coast.

2,400–1,000 BC Bronze Age – metal working with bronze (tin and copper). Passage graves on the mainland and Isles of Scilly. Menhirs and stone circles, notably St Cleer on Bodmin Moor and Nine Maidens near Madron.

1,000 BC Celts arrive.

600–43 BC Bronze replaced by iron for tools and weapons. Trade in tin with the Mediterranean Phoenicians.

43 BC–AD 410 Roman occupation of Britain leaves Cornoui, land of the Cornovii, little affected.

500-600 Invasion of the Anglo-Saxon English.

490 St Piran's Oratory, England's oldest place of Christian worship, is founded.

500–600 the 'Age of the Saints'.

c590 King Arthur supposedly active.

875 Dumgarth, last of the Cornish kings, drowns.

936 Boundary between Anglo-Saxon Wessex and Celtic Cornwall drawn on east bank of River Tamar.

1066 Following the Norman conquest of Britain, Robert of Mortain becomes Earl of Cornwall.

1145 Tintagel castle is begun by Reginald, Earl of Cornwall.

1150 A royal charter recognises the ancient privileges of the 'Stannaries', the four tin-mining areas that make up Cornwall.

1338 Edward, the Black Prince, eldest son of Edward III, made first Duke of Cornwall.

1348–50 The Black Death.

1470s Clampdown on piracy.

1497 Cornish revolt against taxes; 15,000 assemble for a march on London, but are defeated.

1547 Fowey burned in French raid.

1595 French and Spanish attack Mousehole, Newlyn and Penzance.

1619 First lighthouse on the Lizard.

1642–6 English Civil War between Charles I (Cavaliers) and parliamentarians (Roundheads). The parliamentarians are victorious and the king is executed.

1656 Lady Killigrew, notorious woman pirate, siezes Spanish ship at Falmouth.

1660 After the restoration of the monarchy, John Carew of Antony House, a judge at the trial of Charles I, is found guilty of regicide and executed.

1688 Bishop Trelawney is imprisoned in The Tower of London for refusing to recognise Roman Catholicism.

1689 The Falmouth Packet is the first regular sea-going mail service, to La Coruña in Spain. In 1702 it starts a service to the West Indies.

1720s Dolcoath tin mine sunk to a

record depth of 3,300 ft (1,000 m).

1743–98 John Wesley repeatedly visits Cornwall, which becomes predominantly Methodist.

1746 William Cookworthy, a Plymouth chemist, discovers china clay.

1777 Death of Dolly Pentreath, said to be the last Cornish speaker.

1784 William Murdock's Redruth house is first in the world to be lit by gas.

1789 Bread riots in Truro.

1791 Charles Rashleigh constructs Charlestown port to export china clay.

1801 Engineering genius Richard Trevithick drives first passenger-carrying locomotive up Beacon Hill, Camborne.

1809 Portreath Tramroad, Cornwall's first railroad, opens.

1812 Andrew Pears of Mevagissey perfects soap refining. He is the founder of Pears Soap Co.

1817 Miners' safety lamp devised by Sir Humphry Davy of Penzance.

1823 Bude canal opens to transport sand inland.

1829 Treator-born Sir Goldsworthy Gurney drives his steam carriage from London to Bath.

1830s The Great Migration begins, and continues to the end of the century.

1834 Compulsory education introduced in Scilly Isles, ahead of the mainland.

1845 East Wheel Ross mining disaster; 39 killed.

1859 Brunel's Royal Albert Bridge brings railway over the River Tamar. Camborne School of Mines founded.

1871 Flowers first sent from Isles of Scilly to Covent Garden market.

1887 Truro Cathedral, by John Pearson, is completed.

1901 First tranatlantic radio signal sent by Marconi from Cornwall.

1941 Painter Alfred Wallis dies in Madron workhouse.

1953 Prince Charles inherits Duchy of Cornwall.

1961 Tamar road bridge opens.

1964 Penzance–Scilly Isles is Europe's first helicopter passenger service.

1967 Oil tanker *Torrey Canyon* runs aground and pollutes Cornwall's coasts.

1981 Penlee lifeboat tragedy; eight lifeboatmen drown.

1985 Tin crisis as price falls, wiping out Cornish mining industry.

1992 Tate Gallery St Ives opens.

1998 The closure of South Crofty ends 4,000 years of Cornish metal mining.

2000 The Eden Project opens.

2002 National Maritime Museum opens on redeveloped docks in Falmouth.

2004 In August a flash flood devastates Boscastle, but there is no loss of life.

2007 The refurbished Newlyn Gallery completed, and its sister gallery, The Exchange, opens in Penzance.

Map on page 19

1: Saltash to Mount Edgcumbe

Saltash – Cotehele – Gunnislake – Launceston – Trematon Castle – St Germans – Antony House – Mount Edgcumbe

Passing through
Saltash is not the best place to make your base for touring the area, as there is very little accommodation and few places in which to eat. Better to move on towards the coastal resorts that lie a little further west.

Preceding pages: the stunning coast near Land's End
Below: Brunel's bridge
Bottom: beautiful Cotehele House

Nothing has done more to keep Cornwall Cornish than the River Tamar. From its springs at Woolley Barrows, just a few miles from the north Cornish coast, down to Plymouth Sound, it proved an effective barrier against the Romans and the Anglo Saxons, and provided broad waters and landing places for the ships that took away the produce of Cornish mines (copper and tin) and quarries (granite and slate).

SALTASH

Before Brunel took his broad-gauge railway engines over the Royal Albert Bridge in 1859 at **Saltash**, the lowest bridging point 9 miles (15 km) further inland as the crow flies (but many more by water) was Gunnislake. Not until 1961 did a new road bridge join Brunel's, forcing the closure of a ferry that had operated for 700 years. Saltash, by-passed by the A38, rests on its memories, the oldest one embedded in the tiny, Tudor cottage in Culver Road, where Sir Francis Drake's wife, Mary, was born. **Mary Newman's Cottage** can be visited as part of the Heritage Trail (Apr–Sept),

as can Elliott's Grocery Store, a classic old shop (tel: 01752-844846). There have long been plans to turn the station building (abandoned, although some trains still stop here) into a Brunel Heritage Centre, but funds are not yet available.

Stunning views can be had from below the bridge, where 18th-century houses cluster in the steep streets and on the quayside, side by side with modern council housing. The 1780 **Guildhall**, raised on arcaded columns, nudges the parish church with its slate Norman tower.

Star Attraction
● Cotehele House

HEADING UP THE TAMAR

From Saltash, the A388, the major road north, deserts the Tamar, but our route turns off to the right at St Mellion and winds its way through pretty lanes to ★ **Cotehele Quay**; here, evidence of a once-busy trading place is captured in a museum, wharf buildings and the *Shamrock*, the last Tamar sailing barge. There's a National Trust tearoom, and a watermill, cider press and blacksmith's forge are a short walk through the woods. The complex relates to ★★★ **Cotehele House** (NT; open mid-Mar–Oct: Sat–Thurs 11am–4.30pm; garden all year, 10.30am–dusk), a strong contender for the title of most beautiful stately home in the county. Built between 1485 and 1627, this great medieval building, with its rich Flemish and English tapestries, is remarkably unchanged. In the chapel the 15th-century clock, the earliest in England, still ticks today, even though it has neither hands nor pendulum. The lush gardens descend in terraces to the quay past a medieval dovecote, a stew pond (fish pond) and a chapel in the woods.

A short riverside walk passes the picturesque Danescombe Hotel to ★ **Calstock**. The Tamar Valley railway line between Plymouth and Gunnislake ruined Calstock's shipbuilding industry and river trade, but compensated with one of the county's most

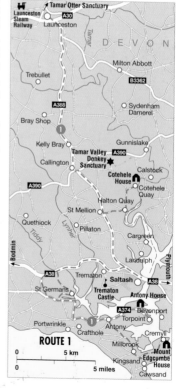

Map on page 19

Below: Launceston Castle
Bottom: Gunnislake Viaduct

attractive branch lines. The views of the river from the viaduct are breathtaking.

New Bridge at **Gunnislake** belies its name, dating from 1520. It was the scene of bitter fighting between Royalists and Roundheads in England's Civil War (1642–46). From riverside quays below the bridge, tin, copper and tungsten were shipped from the intensively mined area of Drakewalls, now recalled only by the ruins of chimneys and engine houses. The village road that climbs steeply from the west bank gives wonderful glimpses of woods and the formidable Morwell Rocks on the Devon side of the river.

WALLED CITY

Northwest of Gunnislake, 14 miles (22 km) along the A388 from Callington, is **Launceston**, Cornwall's only walled town, founded in the 11th century. William the Conqueror gave his half-brother, the Earl of Mortain, the land surrounding a hill site already fortified by Edward the Confessor and commanding the approaches to the west. Within a year the hill was crowned with the castle of Dunheved, a keep on an artificial motte, with bailey, walls and gates enclosing the settlement. Launceston was born, secure from English resistance. Later, the castle became the stronghold of Richard, Earl of Cornwall.

Today, ★ **Launceston Castle** (EH; open
Apr–Jun and Sept: daily 10am–5pm; Jul–Aug:
till 6pm; Oct: till 4pm) sits in grounds immacu-
lately maintained by English Heritage. The steep
ascent to the keep is worthwhile for the astounding views from the top – not only of the town itself
but also over Bodmin Moor and Dartmoor.

Launceston was Cornwall's principal town
until civic power was transferred to Bodmin in
1835. A Victorian revival gave it a town hall and
a guildhall, but its most interesting building is
★★ **St Mary Magdalene**, once the castle chapel
and now the parish church. Built between 1511
and 1524 by Sir Henry Trecarrel, a local
landowner, after he lost both his son and his wife,
it is a work of sculpture as much as architecture,
the external granite walls completely covered
with a host of decorative motifs.

Go out via the North Gate into elegant 18th-
century Castle Street. ★ **Lawrence House** (NT;
open Apr–Sept: Mon–Fri 10.30am–4.30pm), now
a museum, was built in 1753 for a lawyer.

North of the centre is the ★ **Launceston Steam
Railway** (open Easter & Jun–Sept: Sun–Fri; tel:
01566-775665 for exact hours and timetable).
Victorian locomotives, a museum, workshops and
station buffet offer a trip down memory lane.

Animal rescue
Close to Launceston are two
places of interest to animal
lovers and children: the Tamar Valley
Donkey Sanctuary (open Easter–Oct:
daily 10am–5.30pm; Sat & Sun in winter) is just off the A390 near Callington
on the road that leads down to Cotehele, if approached from this direction.

Five miles (8 km) northwest of
Launceston, on the B3254 to Bude, is
the Tamar Otter Sanctuary (open
Easter–Oct: daily 10.30am–6pm;
otter feeding times noon and 3pm;
waterfowl 2.30pm). The Otter Trust
breeds these appealing creatures and
reintroduces them into the wild.
There's a visitor centre and a nature
trail, with lots of wildfowl and deer.

ST GERMANS

Heading back towards Saltash, take the A38 west;
high above a tidal creek of the Lynher River is
Trematon Castle, an important Norman stronghold. It has belonged to the Duchy of Cornwall
since the 14th century and was a favourite retreat
of Edward III's son, the Black Prince (1330–76).
The house and grounds are private, but the gatehouse and keep can be seen from the road.

In Saxon times, the church at ★★ **St Germans**,
reached via a narrow left turn off the A38, was
Cornwall's cathedral. After the bishops moved to
Crediton, and later Exeter, it became an Augus-
tinian priory, and the substantial remains of the
Norman building are now the parish church. The
imposing twin towers of the west front, one an

St Germans church

Map on page 19

Alternative route
Although our route runs via the town of St Germans, both Antony and Mount Edgcumbe houses are signposted to the left further west along the A38, where there is an information point and a large tourist-oriented store on the corner of the A374.

Mount Edgcumbe gardens are a delight in early summer

octagon, are parted by the great west doorway, Cornwall's finest, giving access to an awe-inspiring space within. Part of the priory building is incorporated in the grounds of **Port Eliot**, home of the Eliot family for 400 years. The pretty gabled almshouses in the village date from 1538.

TWO GREAT HOUSES

The road joins the A374 to Torpoint and the Devonport ferry, passing ★★ **Antony House** (NT; open Apr–Oct: Tues–Thur 1.30–5.30pm; also BH Mons & Sun Jun–Aug; woodland garden: Mar–Oct: Tues–Thurs, Sat–Sun 11am–5.30pm), by the River Lynher. Wings of red brick contrast with Pentewan stone and, although a little austere, it is one of the finest early 18th-century houses in Cornwall. Views of the river have been opened up in the 100-acre (40-hectare) park and woodland garden, landscaped by Humphry Repton in the 18th century.

Leaving **Millbrook**, at the head of a tidal creek, a delightful lane follows the waterside to ★ **Mount Edgcumbe House** (open Apr–Sept: Sun–Thur 11am–4.30pm) and the entrance to the Country Park at Cremyll Ferry. The Edgcumbe family virtually abandoned their original home at Cotehele *(see page 19)*, in favour of this new site overlooking Plymouth Sound. The 1550s house Sir Richard Edgcumbe built here was a casualty of World War II, but the County Council bought the burnt-out shell and imaginatively recreated it.

Entrance to the 800-acre (320-hectare) park (open all year: daily) is free; it includes Cornwall's only Grade I listed historic garden, the National Camellia Collection, follies, grottoes, an orangery, a conservatory and a sacred well.

There are dramatic coastal views from walks that lead to **Maker Church**, the tower of which served as a semaphore station in the 18th century. The coastal path soon descends to **Kingsand** and **Cawsand**, separated by a stream. In the early 19th century both subsisted on smuggling, for which their twisting, turning lanes seem to have been specially designed.

2: The South Coast Harbours

**Liskeard – Looe – Polperro – Fowey –
Menabilly – Lostwithiel**

Although its days as an important tin-mining town
are a distant memory, its castle has been replaced
by a war memorial and its canal link with Looe
has long been abandoned, **Liskeard** (on the A38
from Saltash) still has much to offer in the wealth
of its Georgian buildings, second only to Truro. It
was granted a charter by Richard, Earl of Cornwall, in 1240 and prosperity came with the rich
Caradon tin mines. Granite was quarried from the
Moor and there was a flourishing market in wool.

A SHORT TOUR OF THE TOWN

St Martin's Church has little to commend it
except size. The Victorian **Town Hall** is rather
inappropriately Italianate, with a clock tower.
There are imposing stone and slate-hung houses
in The Parade, a Regency **Market Hall** and Stuart House, where Charles I slept for nine nights
during the Civil War (1642–46). Well Lane has
a surprise attraction – although it looks as if it
wants to keep it hidden: in an arched grotto, water,
once believed to have curative properties, spouts
from the 16th-century **Pipe Well**.

Map
on page
25

Star Attraction
● Antony House

*Below: boats on Looe River
Bottom: shopping in Liskeard*

Map on page 25

Below: picturesque Polperro and (bottom) the tiny harbour

UNEXPECTED PLEASURES

Backtrack a few miles and take the B3252 for a lovely drive south to Looe, or carry on, taking the B3254 which hugs the railway and the old Liskeard–Looe Canal as far as St Keyne Station and **Magnificent Music Machines** (open Easter–Oct: daily 10.30am–5pm; tel: 01579-343108). Housed in a water mill, the great Wurlitzer and the other organs strike a fascinating note. A lane opposite climbs to **St Keyne's Well**, famous for giving a person who drank from it mastery over their spouse in marriage.

EAST AND WEST LOOE

A deeply wooded valley joins that of the West Looe River, above the bridge that links East and West Looe, which were both given charters in the 13th century. ★★ **East Looe** is the larger and more commercially important; although its glory has faded, it's an attractive little town. The quays from which ore was loaded onto schooners now throng with visitors, and warehouses have been converted into holiday flats, restaurants and shops. The town's prosperity depends on tourism and on a revival of the fishing industry, whose trawlers line the quay. The 16th-century **Old Guildhall** (open Easter, May–Sept: Sun–Fri 11.30am–4.30pm) houses a museum devoted to fishing and smuggling.

The tangle of narrow streets lined with quaint old houses invites exploration; dozens of cafés and restaurants invite you to try their fresh fish dishes; and **Living from the Sea** (open Easter–Oct: daily), by the fish market, has a shark museum. Boat trips are offered to Fowey and Mevagissey, and moorings are available by the day or week.

Across the bridge in **West Looe**, the 14th-century **Church of St Nicholas** on the quay has had a chequered career as a guildhall, prison, and school. The **Jolly Sailor Inn** looks well adapted to its smuggling history.

POLPERRO

It's a short, scenic drive to ★★★ **Polperro**, which lives up to its reputation as Cornwall's most picturesque fishing village. It may not have inspired great art, but thousands of amateur artists come here to paint. Colour-washed cottages, some more than 300 years old, crowd the steep hillsides converging on a brook that flows fast through the village, under stone bridges into the tiny harbour. Here, the **House on Props**, a 16th-century inn, is poised over the Roman – or some say Saxon – bridge. Some of the cottage gates open onto the roofs of dwellings below. It's easy to see how the fisherfolk were able to conduct their alternative occupation – smuggling.

Cars are banished to the car park near Crumplehorn Mill Inn at the entry to the village. Gypsy-style carts wait to take visitors to the harbour and the Polperro-in-miniature **Model Village and Railway** (open: Easter–Oct: daily from 10am; tel: 01503-272241).

Star Attractions
● East Looe
● Polperro

> **Looe Valley Line**
> The Looe Valley Line (open Mon–Sat, also Sun from mid-Jul–mid-Sept), which the Looe road crosses at Sandplace, was built in order to serve the mines and quarries of Bodmin Moor. Not until 1879 did passengers replace minerals, and it was 1901 before it was connected to the main line.

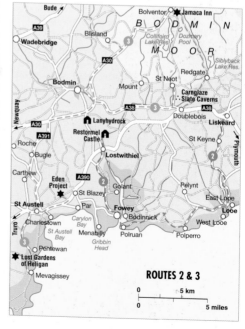

ROUTES 2 & 3

Map
on page
25

The **Heritage Museum of Smuggling and Fishing** (open Easter–Oct: daily 10am–6pm) sits on the quayside, and trips on fishing trawlers are offered from the Harbour Master's office. Take a path up the hillside to enjoy the splendid views.

POLRUAN AND BODINNICK FERRY

Tortuous, narrow lanes, that get very crowded in summer, skirt the coast west to Polruan and Bodinnick Ferry, with a tempting diversion to the church of **Lanteglos-by-Fowey**, a real taste of old Cornwall with slate floors, wagon roofs, carved bench ends and a lantern cross by the south door. **Polruan** is Fowey's poor relation, declining as the town across the estuary prospered. Today it lives on its magnificent views from the pretty cottages above the tiny harbour and passenger ferry. Because of a threat from French marauders in 1457, it has a blockhouse built on the rocks at the shore, the twin of one at Fowey. ★ **Hall Walk**, with panoramic views of Fowey, is reached from Pont Pill Creek and follows the hillside.

Most drivers, however, will follow signs to **Bodinnick Ferry**, where car ferries make the two-minute crossing to Fowey at frequent intervals throughout the day. 'Ferryside', on the waterfront, was once the home of novelist Daphne du Maurier, the author of *Rebecca* and *Jamaica Inn* (*see page 80*). It is still the property of her family.

Fowey's history

Fowey was nationally important seven centuries ago: when London could muster only 25 ships for the Siege of Calais in the Hundred Years' War, Fowey sent 47 ships and 700 men. Given a taste for action, these 'Fowey Gallants' turned pirates and carried on fighting even when the war was declared over. On one of their forays the French were unable to take **Place House**, the seat of the Treffry family, having failed to take account of the feisty resistance of Dame Elizabeth Treffry; although her husband was away fighting in the wars, she took them on and forced them to beat a hasty retreat. Today, the fairy-tale turrets and battlements of the largely 19th-century house provide the town with a peaceful and romantic backdrop.

Fowey – the quay and the King of Prussia inn

FOWEY

Houses huddle daintily around the deep-water harbour at ★★★ **Fowey** (pronounced *Foy*), which calls itself 'Du Maurier Country' (the Du Maurier Centre can be visited, tel: 01726-833616 for details). The Fowey estuary is one of the south coast's best sailing areas, and it has romantic creeks for landlubbers to explore, and some upmarket little shops and galleries for them to spend their money in. The **Fowey River Gallery** (open Mon–Sat 10am–5pm and Sun 11am–4pm in summer) in Fore Street, next to the Georgian Post Office building, has a good reputation.

Above **Readymoney Cove**, at the end of the Esplanade, Henry VIII built St Catherine's Castle. Here, surmounted by a massive stone crown, is the mausoleum of the wealthy Rashleigh family; their town house, now the Ship Hotel, stands by the gate of ★ **St Fimbarrus Church**. This commanding, 14th-century building has the second highest tower in Cornwall and a Norman font, a survivor from an earlier church on the site.

In Trafalgar Square, little **Fowey Museum** (open May–Sept: Mon–Fri 10am–5pm) has an interesting history: built in 1792, it incorporates a 14th-century chapel, did time as a prison and now commemorates Fowey's maritime past.

Facing the quay is the **King of Prussia** inn raised on granite columns, between which a market was held. Queen Victoria visited Fowey with her consort in 1846, and there is Albert Quay to prove it (with the Victoria Tea Rooms on the corner). Novelist Sir Arthur Quiller-Couch *(see page 81)* came here from Bodmin in 1892, and stayed for the rest of his life in 'The Haven' at Whitehouse Point. In writing about Troy Town and its people, he portrayed a thinly disguised Fowey.

POLRIDMOUTH COVE AND MENABILLY

★ **Polridmouth Cove** (pronounced Pridmouth) can be reached from the Fowey–St Austell road

Star Attraction
● Fowey

*Below: St Fimbarrus Church
Bottom: Fowey's deep-water harbour*

Map on page 25

and a small car park. A short walk downhill is the cove and a landlocked pool below the woods of ★ **Menabilly**. To this place of haunted beauty Daphne du Maurier came in 1943, leaving reluctantly 24 years later when it was reclaimed by the Rashleighs. At the crossroads beyond is the 6th-century standing stone inscribed with the name *Drustanus*, lending credibility to the legend of Tristan and Iseult. On the Lostwithiel road lies **Castle Dore**, the prehistoric earthwork where the tragic lovers are reputedly buried.

Du Maurier country
The area is rich with du Maurier connections. Daphne had a romantic wedding, setting off from the home of her father (the actor, Gerald du Maurier) at Bodinnick by boat to Lanteglos Church, near the head of nearby Pont Pill.

A sleepy young inhabitant of the moor

LOSTWITHIEL

It's difficult now to believe that ★ **Lostwithiel** (reached via the B3269 from Fowey, or the faster A390) was once Cornwall's capital, the centre of the tin industry and a flourishing port. Yet its historic presence is still there, half-hidden in this serene, French-looking place beside the River Fowey. In Quay Street are the remains of Stannary Court, the 14th-century **Duchy Palace**, which served as the Hall of the Exchequer, Shire Hall and prison. There are numerous attractive 18th-century buildings, including the **Guildhall Museum** (open Easter–Sept: Mon–Sat 10.30am–12.30pm, 2.30–4.30pm) in Fore Street, evoking life during the 18th and 19th centuries.

Fascinating alleys, called opes, connect the tightly built streets, centred on **St Bartholomew's Church**, with a 14th-century lantern spire that owes its style more to Brittany than to Cornwall. It survived a bomb blast during the Civil War (1642–46), when Parliamentarians used drastic measures to dislodge Royalists from the tower.

The wooded valley above the bridges is commanded by 13th-century ★★ **Restormel Castle** (EH: open Apr–Jun and Sept: daily 10am–5pm; Jul–Aug: till 6pm; Oct: till 4pm), a stronghold of the Earls of Cornwall. The circular keep over the artificially steepened hill and a deep moat (now dry) was regarded as a perfect military solution. Fought over in the Civil War, it survives as an impressive ruin and the grounds make a delightful picnic spot.

3: Bodmin to Mevagissey

Bodmin – Loveny Valley – St Austell – Eden Project – Charlestown – Heligan – Mevagissey

Bodmin Moor is a place to be treated with respect. Covering Cornwall's backbone in a granite blanket, it was home and shelter to the county's earliest inhabitants, and everywhere on the rock-strewn uplands are prehistoric stone circles, huts, barrows and medieval fields. The moor has a character quite unlike its counterpart in Devon, neither as large nor as elevated as Dartmoor and contrasting strongly with the granite moorland north of St Austell (*see page 33*).

GATEWAY TO THE MOOR

★**Bodmin**, gateway to the Moor, is reached via the A30 from Launceston or Truro, or the B3269 from Lostwithiel. It was on the old trade route from Ireland to the continent, and attracted 5th-century Christians who often broke their lengthy journeys here. Guron was the first, as evidenced by his holy well in St Petroc's churchyard and a roadside fountain. St Petroc, Cornwall's senior saint, followed in the 6th century, founding a priory of which only fragments remain. The 15th-century ★ **Church of St Petroc** (open Apr–Sept:

Star Attraction
● Restormel Castle

Below: Celtic remains on Bodmin Moor
Bottom: Restormel Castle

Map on page 25

Map on page 25

Below: Bodmin Jail is now a museum
Bottom: enigmatic stone circle

daily 11am–3pm) has an important treasure: the cask that contained his relics. It has twice been stolen and returned, but without its contents. St Petroc's is Cornwall's largest church and its beautiful Norman font, supported by angels, is probably the best in the county. The church has good acoustics and is used as a venue for concerts.

EXPLORING THE TOWN

This sensible, hardworking town lost much of its administrative importance when its county town status was lost to Truro. The imposing, 19th-century **Shire Hall** (housing a helpful tourist office) stands in Mount Folly Square. The Tudor guildhall next door is now **Bodmin Museum** (open Apr–Oct: Mon–Fri 10.30am–4.30pm, Sat 2.30–4.30pm; free); it contains a manual fire engine, a Cornish kitchen and world war memorabilia, but won't detain you for long.

Some of the nation's most precious possessions, such as the Domesday Book (1086) and the crown jewels, were kept for safety during World War I in **Bodmin Jail** (open daily 10am–dusk; 'paranormal walks' on specific dates, tel: 01208 76292), in Berrycombe Road, signposted off the St Austell road. Public executions were held here from the 1850s to 1862; you can visit the dungeons for more gruesome details.

The town's close links with the Cornish Infantry regiment are illustrated in the **Duke of Cornwall's Light Infantry Museum** (open Mon–Fri 10.30am–5pm and Sun in Jul–Aug) in the former Victoria Barracks on the Lostwithiel Road.

Almost opposite is the station of the ★ **Bodmin and Wenford Steam Railway** (open Easter–Oct and Christmas/New Year: 10am–5.30pm; tel: 0845-1259678 for details). It has a refreshment room and souvenir shop and offers special events as well as a nostalgic 6-mile (9-km) trip.

LANHYDROCK

Bodmin's bypass (to the south) skirts the 30-acre (12-hectare) parkland of ★★ **Lanhydrock** (NT; open mid-Mar–Sept: Tues–Sun 11am–5.30pm; Oct: until 5pm; park and gardens: all year: daily). The Robartes family, lived here for more than 300 years, and the National Trust has managed to retain a lived-in atmosphere. Special highlights are the long gallery with an astounding plasterwork ceiling; and the eight-room kitchen complex which demonstrates what life 'downstairs' was like.

Spring arrives with magnolias, rhododendrons and azaleas in the formal gardens laid out around the church behind the house. It's a 600-yd/metre walk from car park to house, but vintage cars will drive you there or back for £1 (there is parking for people with disabilities close to the house).

THE MOOR

The bogs and heather of Bodmin Moor reach down the Loveny Valley to the road to Liskeard and **Carnglaze Slate Caverns** (tours: Mon–Sat 10am–5pm; Aug: till 8pm; tel: 01579-320251), with the most beautiful pool hidden in its depths.

St Neot, higher up the valley, has royal connections. The saint was King Alfred's brother and his church is a palace of light and colour; 15 windows shine with stained glass that is among the finest in England. The saint's Holy Well, in the meadow nearby, supposedly supported him on his quota of one fish a day.

Star Attraction
● Lanhydrock

Cheesewring
Near Siblyback Lake on Bodmin Moor you will find the extraordinary granite tower called Cheesewring, where an 18th-century hermit and mathematician, Daniel Gumb, carved his name as well as Euclid's 47th theorem on a slab of rock.

Cheesewring – there's a theorem carved on the rock

At Doublebois, a road forks left to join the Fowey River at ★ **Golitha Falls** in a National Nature Reserve and, passing **King Doniert's Stone**, with its Latin inscription to Dungarth, King of Cornwall, allows access to the **Siblyback Lake**, where there are water sports and those with a day ticket may fish for trout. Just south is **St Cleer**, with a chapel over a roadside holy well insensitively crowded by modern development. ★ **Trethevy Quoit**, easily accessible nearby, is a magnificent example of a Neolithic tomb.

Still following the river upstream, **Dozmary Pool** lies to the left in the wildest part of the moor. In Alfred Lord Tennyson's poetic vision, it was here that King Arthur's sword was consigned to the waters after his death. The legendary 17th-century Cornish rogue, Jan Tregeagle, for sins committed while he was steward at Lanhydrock, was condemned after his death to empty Dozmary Pool using a limpet shell with a hole in it.

At Bolventor is **Jamaica Inn**, which does its best to live up to the character conferred on it by Daphne du Maurier's romantic novel. The slate-hung Georgian buildings look as if they could still harbour smugglers *(see page 94 for accommodation details)* and there is a small smugglers' museum attached.

The inn Daphne du Maurier made famous

LEAVING THE MOOR

To the right of the A30, as you leave the moor, is **Blisland**. The Norman church (John Betjeman's favourite), with a brilliantly coloured screen and barrel roof, sits beside the only village green in Cornwall, beside an inn, a manor house and some cottages. Bypassing Bodmin, the A391 plunges into the much-abused landscape of china clay country *(see box)*. At Bugle, a diversion can be made to ★ **Roche Rock**, a granite outcrop capped with the 15th-century St Michael's Chapel and a hermit's cell below, reached by a ladder.

Wheal Martyn China Clay Museum (open Easter–Oct: daily 10am–6pm; Nov–Mar: Wed–Sun 10am–4pm; tel: 01726-850362), set in a disused china clay works at Carthew, 2 miles

Star Attraction
● Eden Project

(3 km) north of St Austell, and extensively refurbished in 2004, brings the industry vividly to life.

St Austell is the area's main town. In the old quarter, the Market Hall and tower of Holy Trinity Church offer good photo opportunities. Elsewhere are some fine old buildings, such as the White Hart Hotel and the **St Austell Brewery Visitor Centre** in Trevarthian Road (open Mon–Fri; for tours, tel: 01726-66022).

THE EDEN PROJECT

At Bodelva, sign-posted from the A391 before you reach St Austell, is Cornwall's most spectacular and well-marketed attraction, the ★★★ **Eden Project** (open Apr–Oct: daily 9.30am–6pm; Nov–Mar: 10am–4.30pm). This Millennium project, a 35-acre (14-hectare) site in a disused clay pit, has transformed one of the few unattractive areas of Cornwall into a place everybody wants to visit. It's a vast global garden, incorporating huge, dome-shaped conservatories, called biomes, that resemble a surreal space station made of bubble-wrap.

There's a **Humid Tropics Biome**, the world's largest greenhouse, full of tropical plants, with 'cool rooms' for those who find the heat and humidity too much. Roofs let through UV light, so you may need sunscreen and hats on sunny days.

> **Lunar landscape**
> Approaching St Austell you will see that the landscape has been transformed by the extraction of china clay, with stark white spoil heaps and water-filled pools giving it a lunar appearance. Not pretty, but the industry used to be a mainstay of the economy. It owes its origin to a Plymouth chemist, William Cookworthy, who discovered the clay near Helston in 1746. The exceptional purity of the clay made it ideal for the production of porcelain and paper, and demand encouraged investment in the construction of ports like Par and Charlestown.

The Eden Project – a vast global garden

Map on page 25

In the giant **Warm Temperate Biome**, recreating the landscapes of the Mediterranean, California and South Africa, and the **Roofless Biome** (outdoor zone), the crops – from olives and grapes indoors to hemp and sunflowers outside – are maturing nicely. A Semi-Arid Biome is planned, when funding is available. It is a place with serious environmental ambitions and there's a strong emphasis on education. Hourly environmental lectures are conducted in the biomes, and a new Foundation Building is home to the science, horticulture and creative departments.

There's an informative Visitor Centre, a large shop and three good restaurants, with lots of outdoor seating. On arrival you will be shepherded into one of the tiers of car parks, 'fruit coded' from cherries and plums near the top to apples at the bottom; a park and ride system operates from the higher levels. There's also a little 'landtrain' that ferries people between the Visitor Centre and and the biomes. If you come by bike *(see page 88 for bike hire)* you pay a reduced entry price. For further information, and details of summer concerts, tel: 01726-811911, or visit www.edenproject.com

Ways to enter Eden

The Eden Branchline bus service connects the Eden Project with St Austell station, and there are daily buses from Newquay. Tourist information centres and many hotels sell advance tickets (only groups can book in advance at the project) for the same price as they are on the door. This enables you to get in faster on busy days. It doesn't avoid queues to get into the car parks but these are fewer since the system has been streamlined.

CHARLESTOWN

Take the A390 past St Austell and follow signs to the port of ★★ **Charlestown**, the brainchild of

A green man in the gardens of Heligan

Charles Rashleigh of Menabilly. Dug out of the beach in the 1790s, it has a granite-lined entrance and was intended for the shipment of both copper and tin. Today it handles china clay and also sometimes caters for film crews. An inn or two, terraces of granite Georgian houses, stores and fish cellars provide the setting, and the **Charlestown Shipwreck and Heritage Centre** (open Mar–Oct: daily 10am–5pm; children under 12 free) fills in the town's historic background on both land and sea.

Star Attractions
● **Charlestown**
● **Lost Gardens of Heligan**

THE LOST GARDENS OF HELIGAN

The B3273 towards Mevagissey takes you to another of Cornwall's greatest attractions, ★★ **The Lost Gardens of Heligan** (open Mar–Oct: daily 10am–6pm; Nov–Feb: 10am–5pm; www.heligan.com). The Victorian gardens became completely overgrown after the house was converted into a military hospital, and decades of neglect were compounded by the 1988 hurricane. The award-winning grounds are now beautifully restored. There are boardwalks through a subtropical area called The Jungle, lakes, wetlands and woodlands in the Lost Valley, and vegetables and exotic fruits in the walled garden. Be aware that there is little shelter if the weather is bad.

MEVAGISSEY

Pilchards were the mainstay of ★ **Mevagissey**, about a mile downhill from the Heligan turning. 'Mevagissey Ducks', as they were called, were once salted in barrels to victual the Royal Navy, and they supported a fishing fleet that both filled the large double harbour and fed a flourishing community. But there is life after pilchards, and Mevagissey has adapted well to entertaining its many visitors. It is rather appealingly tatty, with lots of fish and chips and ice creams, that do not detract from its picturesque character.

The little **Mevagissey Museum** (open Easter–Oct: daily 11am–5pm), housed in an 18th-century boat yard on East Quay, has an interesting collection of old photos and marine artefacts.

Mevagissey Lighthouse

Maps below & page 38

4: Truro to Falmouth

Truro – Tresillian – St Mawes – Falmouth

★★ **Truro** is unquestionably a city, albeit a small one. Its new Crown Courts (designed by the same architects that gave St Ives the Tate) have pushed it even further ahead of Bodmin. Commercial priorities have developed much of the town centre, not always in a sympathetic way, and a ring road separates Truro's heart from its shipping heritage. In recent years a handful of new restaurants and interesting shops have opened in the centre.

Changing fortunes

The Normans were Truro's first settlers but the name Castle Hill is all that survives of their fort. Trade in tin brought prosperity and, having been granted a charter by Edward I in 1307, Truro became one of Cornwall's four regulators of the mining industry. The town's fortunes suffered a reversal as the market in tin fluctuated, and it wasn't until the 18th-century copper boom that the town thrived again. With the arrival of the railway in 1859, Truro's distinguished future was secured.

CATHEDRAL AND CITY HALL

In 1880, four years after the diocese of Truro was created, the ★★ **Cathedral** ❶ was begun, the first to be built in England since St Paul's. Its triple towers and spires soar above the surrounding rooftops. John Loughborough Pearson built it in French Gothic style after demolishing the 16th-century parish church of St Mary, except for the south aisle, which he incorporated into the new building. The vaulted interior is elegant but also austere; the stained glass is considered the finest of its era in England – the three rose windows are particularly impressive; and there is a wonderful carved reredos. Opposite the entrance are the **Assembly Rooms and Theatre**. Sadly, Truro's best building is only skin-deep: the 1772 interior no longer exists.

In nearby Boscawen Street, the **City Hall** ❷ houses the splendid Hall for Cornwall, a venue for concerts, theatre, dance and

Map of Truro with locations including Truro Station, Victoria Gardens, Royal Cornwall Museum and Art Gallery ❸, Cathedral ❶, City Hall ❷, Royal Cornwall Hospital, and streets. Scale: 0 – 400 m / 0 – 400 yards. TRURO

light entertainment. Opposite, the ancient Coinage Hall has a pizzeria on the ground floor and the idiosyncratic **Charlotte's Tea Rooms**, surrounded by rooms full of antiques, upstairs.

Beginning beside the City Hall is **Lemon Street**, which broadens into one of the most complete Georgian streets in England. The Lemon Street Market contains some good fresh food shops, as well as gift shops, cafés and an art gallery. On the other side of Boscawen Street, the past is well documented in the ★ **Royal Cornwall Museum and Art Gallery** ❸ (open Mon–Sat 10am–5pm) in River Street, the best museum in Cornwall. As well as local artefacts, from the Stone Age to the present, there are Greek and Roman exhibits and an Egyptian Room containing an unwrapped, splendidly preserved mummy and two decorated coffins.

THE ROSELAND PENINSULA

From Truro, the tree-shaded riverside road down the left bank of the River Truro climbs to the Heron Inn and the hanging gardens of ★ **Malpas**, with enchanting views of river and creek and quiet anchorages, once active with shipbuilding.

To reach the Roseland Peninsula, backtrack on the A390 and turn off just after **Tresillian** on the A3078. The road goes through **Tregony**, a seaport until the 17th century when the River Fal silted up with mush from the tin mines and clay pits. It's an attractive village, with balconied almshouses supported on pillars. From the bridge, the road into the **Roseland Peninsula** begins a meandering course through narrow lanes.

A left turn leads to the miniature fishing cove of ★ **Portloe** where a stream reaches the beach from beneath the Lugger Inn. The villagers of ★ **Veryan**, inland from Portloe, seem to have been rather sensitive to the powers of the devil. Determined that he should find no corner in which to hide, they built the five round, thatched cottages that command the roads into the village, capping each one with a cross. For good measure, there are two holy wells. Down below the church of St Symphorian is a beautiful water garden.

Star Attraction
● Truro

Truro's cathedral towers soar above the rooftops

Map below

Unusual gardens

A side trip from Tresillian (see map below) takes you to two interesting gardens: Probus (open Mar–Oct: daily 10am–5pm; Nov–Feb: 10am–4pm) is a fascinating experimental place, with a winter area, a low-allergen garden and lots of vegetables and fruit.

At Trewithen (open Mar–Sept: Mon–Sat 10am–4.30pm; Apr–May: daily), there is a magnificent collection of rhododendrons, camellias, magnolias and rare shrubs. Many plants propagated here are for sale.

ST MAWES

Back on the A3078, take the left fork as you approach ★ **St Mawes** and follow the coastal road, past villas with lush, Mediterranean-style gardens, to the harbour. This is a smart little resort, with yachts bobbing in the bay. Ferries bustle in from Falmouth across Carrick Roads, and yacht owners carouse in the Victory Inn. A few steps above the inn is a holy well. Pretty cottages, some thatched, line the seafront to the perfectly preserved **St Mawes Castle** (EH; open Apr–Sept: Sun–Fri 10am–5pm; Oct: 10am–4pm; Nov–Mar: Fri–Mon 10am–4pm). Henry VIII built it in 1543, together with Pendennis, to defend the Carrick Roads and Truro against attack from the sea.

Leaving the village, take a left turn to ★ **St Just-in-Roseland**, where the lych gate of the church frames what is possibly Cornwall's most beautiful view. Reflected in St Just Pool, the 13th-century church makes a pleasing composition.

TRELISSICK GARDENS

The road back to Tregony invites exploration of backwaters: **Ruan Lanihorn**, which once had wharves on the River Fal; and ★ **St Michael Penkevil**, the church and estate cottages clustered round the gates of Tregothnan, seat of the Boscawens, Earls of Falmouth. However, we take the more direct route to Trelissick and Falmouth on the B3289 from St Just, and board the King Harry Ferry which makes the short trip across the Fal at 20-minute intervals (tel: 01872-862312 for details).

Trelissick House, Grecian-style with a columned portico, is private but

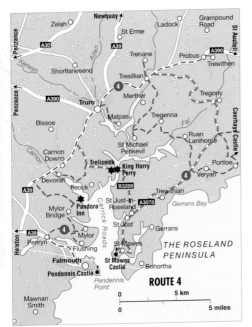

ROUTE 4

0 .... 5 km

0 .... 5 miles

★★ **Trelissick Gardens** are open to the public (NT; open mid-Feb–Oct: daily 10.30am–5.30pm; Nov–Christmas and Jan: 11am–4pm; woodland walk all year: daily till dusk). Among the National Trust's finest in Cornwall, the gardens cover 25 acres (10 hectares) and are famous for hydrangeas and camellias. Surrounding them, oak and beech woods reach down to the River Fal. In summer, ferries run from Falmouth to the gardens.

Star Attractions
● **Trelissick Gardens**
● **Falmouth**

DEVORAN TO PENRYN

At ★ **Devoran** on Restronguet Creek (B3289 from Trelissick) are the grass-covered wharves and converted stores of a ghost port. Once connected by tramline with the mining area of Redruth, exporting minerals and importing coal, it survives on the beauty of its situation.

Lower down the creek is thatched **Pandora Inn**, named after the vessel that brought back Captain Bligh after the mutiny on the *Bounty*. ★ **Mylor**, open to Carrick Roads, is excellent for yachting, and moorings fill the creek. The church of St Mylor still stands, thanks to the support of Cornwall's largest cross, 7ft (2 metres) of which are embedded in the ground. The church has many attractive features: a belfry, two Norman doorways, and an Elizabethan pulpit.

Round Trefusis Point, facing Falmouth, is **Flushing**, reputed to have England's mildest climate. It gained its name in the 17th century when Dutch engineers, working on Falmouth's quays, settled here; their influence can still be seen in the tall houses lining the creek-side High Street.

In the 13th century **Penryn** was a seat of religious learning, then a major port, which declined as Falmouth grew. The granite and slate-hung buildings now enjoy Conservation Area status.

Trelissick Garden is one of the finest in Cornwall

FALMOUTH

★★ **Falmouth** started as a twinkle in Sir Walter Raleigh's eye. When he dropped anchor in the cove below Pendennis Castle on his return from Guiana in the late 16th century, he decided it

Map on page 38

Below: Pendennis Castle
Bottom: the National Maritime Museum has become a popular family attraction

would make a good harbour. He found Sir John Killigrew, the local lord, very responsive, and the development of the village of Pennycomequick was decided. By 1663 it had become Falmouth.

Falmouth's importance grew with its 1661 Charter. The impressive church of **King Charles the Martyr** (open most days), at the top of busy Church Street, was built at the Killigrews' expense a year later, and the port was appointed Headquarters of the Royal Mail Packet Service.

The arrival of the railway in 1863 to serve the new docks heralded the town's development as a holiday resort, and increased the need for accommodation, which began in Cliff Road, above the southern beaches, where terraces stretch away to Swanpool. Between the beaches and the station, quiet roads are lined with hotels, guesthouses, villas and gardens, the most lovely of which are **Gyllyngdune Gardens**. Signposted from the seafront, paths lead into a sunken area planted with exotic trees and shrubs.

There are 450 years of military history to be explored at ★ **Pendennis Castle** (EH; open Apr–Sept: daily 10am–5pm; Oct–Mar: 10am–4pm). It takes in a Tudor gun deck, underground tunnels and a World War II observation post. Pendennis was built by Henry VIII to protect the estuary from the French – a threat which never materialised. It was the last castle to surrender

to parliamentary forces in the Civil War. Encircling the headland is ★ **Castle Drive**, which must be the most scenic in the West Country (follow the brown 'Scenic Route' signs). A huge new leisure pool and fitness centre, called Ships and Castles, looms to the right of the road.

THE QUAYS AND THE CENTRE

In Arwenack Street, running parallel to the sea, the dilapidated **Custom House**, with imposing Greek Doric columns, fronts Custom House Quay, where pub tables stand beside a small fishing harbour. From here, and from **Prince of Wales Pier**, ferries cross to St Mawes and Flushing, and make extended trips to Trelissick and up the River Fal to Malpas and, if the tide's right, to Truro.

Continue along Arwenack Street, lined with shops and restaurants, past the church and up to **The Moor**, Falmouth's municipal heart. Above the library, ★ **Falmouth Art Gallery** (open Mon–Sat 10am–5pm; free) has a permanent display of Victorian and Edwardian paintings and some good temporary exhibitions. Across The Moor, the 111 stone steps of Jacob's Ladder climb the hillside to a pub of the same name. Follow the harbour still further, instead of turning inland, and you will eventually come to the Yacht Marina.

THE MARITIME MUSEUM

Falmouth is not a wealthy town, but it is undergoing a revival, with the redeveloped quayside site, **Discovery Quay**. The sophisticated new ★★★ **National Maritime Museum Cornwall** (open daily 10am–5pm; www.nmmc.co.uk), dominating the waterfront, is a stunning structure, with a floor-to-ceiling glass viewing gallery. There are lots of hands-on displays, a huge collection of boats of all kinds, and a chance to see traditional boat builders at work, as well as changing exhibitions, and fantastic views over the harbour and town from the 95-m (29-m) tower. The museum opened in September 2002 and was voted Cornwall's Family Attraction of the Year in 2003.

Star Attraction
● **Falmouth National Maritime Museum**

Leisurely age
Above Gyllyngdune Gardens, on Melvill Road, stands the Princess Pavilion, its verandah hung with flowering baskets. The café, theatre, and the original Edwardian bandstand and greenhouse hark back to another age, but the pavilion is still very much in use today, with a bar and café and a full summer programme of musical events and theatrical performances (tel: 01326- 211222).

A view of Falmouth

Map on page 43

5: Helford to the Lizard

Helford – Glendurgan – Mawgan – Lizard Point – Helston – Loe Pool

The Helford River, thrusting westwards, almost detaches the Lizard from the rest of Cornwall. From its east coast estuary, this yachting-friendly river cuts through rich woodland and sends inviting creeks through villages. In dramatic contrast, the plateau stretching to Lizard Point, the southernmost part of England, offers beauty of a different kind. Early in the year the downland blazes gold with gorse and in autumn with pink heather – known as Cornish heath. To the east the rock breaks, twists and scatters in magnificent cliff scenery, its fishing coves isolated down steep and narrow lanes. After Lizard Point is turned, the unrivalled coast to Mullion gives way to the beaches of Mount's Bay.

GLORIOUS GARDENS

Leaving Falmouth via the popular beach of Swanpool, the road to Mawnan Smith is joined to visit two more wonderful gardens. The first is **★★ Glendurgan Garden** (NT; open mid-Feb–Oct: Tues–Sat & BH Mons 10.30am–5.30pm). Rare, exotic and subtropical plants fill the south-

Trebah is a lush and exotic garden

facing slopes of this wooded valley. A laurel maze, originally planted in 1833, has been renewed. An unexpected surprise awaits where the park reaches the Helford River: a tiny group of cottages that comprises the hamlet of **Durgan**.

The neighbouring garden, ★★ **Trebah** (open daily 10.30am–5pm), was first planted in the 1840s in a steeply wooded ravine running down to the river. At its head is a pool containing koi carp, and below are water gardens and a stream falling in cascades to the beach. Hydrangeas, rhododendrons and magnolias provide colour, and palms, tree ferns and giant gunnera the exotic background.

OYSTERS AND SEALS

A creek is skirted to **Porth Navas**, where the Duchy of Cornwall has an oyster farm, and where the south-going B3291 is joined to reach the tiny village of **Gweek** at the head of the Helford River. Once the port for the export of tin from Helston and the import of timber, Gweek suffered the fate of other Cornish inland ports when the river choked with silt. Now it attracts small pleasure craft.

Gweek is home to the **National Seal Sanctuary** (open daily 10am, closing times vary; tel: 01326-221361), which offers the heartening spectacle of rescued seals and sea lions cared for and returned to the wild after convalescence. Feeding times, at regular intervals throughout the day, are what children love.

Turn left over the bridge and left through **Mawgan**. Among the monuments in the church are those to the Vyvyans of **Trelowarren** (open Apr–Sept: daily

The maze at Glendurgan Garden

ROUTE 5

Map
on page
43

11am–5pm), situated in parkland above a long wooded valley. The house still has 15th-century elements. There's a pretty Gothic revival chapel added by Sir Richard Vyvyan in the 18th century, and a gallery devoted to the Cornwall Crafts Association. The woodland walk takes in an Iron Age underground chamber and a Victorian folly.

HELFORD AND COVERACK

Signposted through Manaccan is ★ **Helford**, which has banished cars to a hilltop park. A walk past gardens and colour-washed cottages crosses a bridge and ends by the thatched Shipwright's Arms. Daphne du Maurier's Frenchman's Creek is at the end of a road to Kestle nearby.

A minor southbound road (joining the B3294 for the last stretch) drops down to pretty little ★ **Coverack**. Still with a fleet of working boats, the tiny fishing village with thatched, white-washed cottages is delightful.

Back on the B3293, which climbs to the Goonhilly Downs, standing among the hut circles and burial mounds of prehistory, are the satellite-tracking dishes of British Telecom's **Goonhilly Earth Station** (open Feb–Mar: Tues–Sun 11am–4pm; Apr–May and Oct: daily 10am–5pm; Jun–Sept: daily 10am–6pm; tel: 0800-679593). The Visitors' Centre offers virtual tours and unusual interactive displays.

Now take the road that runs through serpentine rock country to Kuggar. The picturesque route descends along a gorge beside a cascading stream.

Goonhilly Earth Station

GETTING TO THE POINT

Many of the thatched cottages in ★ **Cadgwith**, at the road's end, down hill from Ruan Minor, are built of the black and green mottled serpentine rock. Two tiny coves are separated by a rocky viewpoint, the Todden. A pub and old pilchard cellars complete the picture. The B3083 runs straight down the peninsula to **Lizard**, England's most southerly village, where souvenir shops sell items made from the serpentine rock.

The **Lizard Lighthouse**, signposted from the village centre, was begun by Sir John Killigrew of Falmouth in 1619, but the present buildings date from 1752. Coal, then oil, was used to power the lamps; now the beam, thrown more than 20 miles (32 km), is powered by electricity.

Star Attraction
● Kynance Cove

KYNANCE COVE

Leaving the B3083, you reach ★★ **Kynance Cove** on the Lizard's west coast. It is an unforgettable sight at low tide, with the golden sands and the green, red and purple of the serpentine set against the Prussian blue of the sea. All the rocks have names, some of which are sinister, like Man-o'-War, while the caves have curiously domestic names: Kitchen, Parlour and Dressing Room.

In **Mullion**, on the B3296, St Melanus Church is noted for its 16th-century bench-end carvings. **Mullion Cove** has long defied fierce southwesterly gales but climate change and rising sea levels put its future at risk. To the north, before Poldhu Cove, an obelisk on the cliff records the transmission of the first wireless signals across the Atlantic, sent by Guglielmo Marconi in 1901.

A cliff path skirts a golf course to reach Gunwalloe, or else the main road must be taken for a left-hand turn to ★ **Church Cove**. This remote spot has only ever served a few fishermen, yet

> **Unsung heroes**
> Like all the seaside villages, Cadgwith owes a great debt to the volunteers who man the lifeboat. The little port's finest hour was when the lifeboat helped in the World War II evacuation of Dunkirk.
> The lifeboats here have some back-up: at Culdrose, near Helston, the Royal Navy's air station and Europe's biggest helicopter base answers round-the-clock calls from vessels in distress and undertakes the most dangerous cliff rescues.

Lizard Point, the most southerly spot in England

Map on page 43

a church has stood here since the 14th century. The cove is rich with smuggling legends, and a pirate's treasure is reputed to be buried here.

FLAMBARDS VILLAGE AND HELSTON

Back to the A3083 and, as Helston is approached, you come to ★★ **The Flambards Experience** (open Apr–Oct: daily 10am–5pm), in landscaped gardens at Culdrose Manor. A popular family day out, it includes a recreated Victorian village and a funfair with a log flume and roller coaster rides.

★★ **Helston** is a bustling market town that comes alive on 8 May when it celebrates Flora Day *(see page 82)*. Created a coinage town for tin by Edward I, Helston's old weighing hall was in Coinagehall Street where its successor, the 1839 granite Guildhall, now stands.

Behind, in Old Butter Market, the ★ **Helston Folk Museum** (open Mon–Sat 10am–5pm), portrays West Cornish life past and present. From here, Church Street dips and rises to Georgian **St Michael's**, a church rebuilt on the profits of tin by the Earl of Godolphin. Water runs down open conduits in Coinagehall Street past the 17th-century ★**Blue Anchor Inn**, distinguished by its thatched roof and by the quality of the home-brewed beer.

★★ **Loe Pool** lies just south of Helston, in the heart of the Penrose Estate. It was originally the estuary of the River Cober which, in the 13th century, became blocked at its seaward end by sand and silt. Today the estate and pool are in the care of the National Trust; there are numerous walking paths through the lovely countryside.

TWO HIDDEN TREASURES

Northwest of Helston, on the B3302, is **Trevarno Gardens and National Museum of Gardening** (open daily 10.30am–4.30pm), a plantsman's paradise, with a picturesque lake and Victorian boathouse. A left turn off the B3302 leads to the beautiful Tudor **Godolphin House** (open Apr–Jun: Wed–Thurs and Sun 10am–4pm; Jul–Sept: Tues–Fri and Sun 10am–4pm).

Poldark Mine

At Wendron, on the B3297 2 miles (3 km) north of Helston, you can step back in time at the Poldark Mine (open Apr & Jul–Aug: daily 10am–5.30pm; May–Jun, Sept–Oct: Sun–Fri; last underground tour 4pm; site admission free, charge for tours). The mine was closed in 1820, but its working days and conditions have been recreated. There are workshops and amusements on site. Winston Graham's popular *Poldark* novels, set in the 19th-century Cornish mining communities, made the name familiar.

Machinery in working order at Poldark Mine

6: Land's End Peninsula

Penzance – St Michael's Mount – Land's End – Zennor

Sunny, south-facing ★★ **Penzance** is superbly situated in the embrace of Mount's Bay, with the grandeur of St Michael's Mount its focal point. It is one of the warmest places in Britain, with frost and snow almost non-existent. It is the gateway to the Land's End Peninsula, and has air and sea services to the Isles of Scilly *(see page 90)*.

HISTORICAL BACKGROUND

Mentioned in the Domesday Book and granted a weekly market by Edward III, Penzance first claimed attention in 1595 when Spanish galleons appeared in the bay and the nearby villages of Paul, Mousehole and Newlyn were sacked and burned. Despite opposition mustered by local landowner, Sir Francis Godolphin, Penzance was left in ruins. After rising phoenix-like from the

Star Attractions
- **Flambards Village**
- **Helston**
- **Penzance**

Fishing boats still put out to sea from Penzance

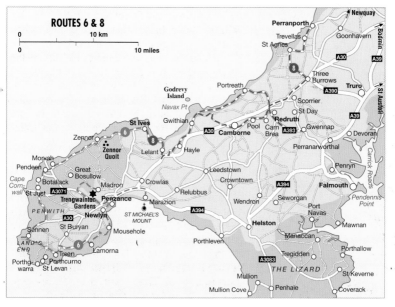

ROUTES 6 & 8

0   10 km
0   10 miles

Newquay
Perranporth
Trevellas   Goonhavern
St Agnes
A30
8
Three Burrows
Portreath   Truro
A390
Godrevy Island   Scorrier
Navax Pt   St Day
St Ives   Gwithian   Pool   Carn   Redruth   A39
Zennor   6   8   A30   Camborne   Brea A393   Gwennap   Devoran
Zennor Quoit   Lelant   Hayle   Perranarworthal
Morvah   Great   Leedstown   Penryn
Pendeen   Bosullow   Crowlas   Crowntown   Falmouth
Cape Corn-   Botallack   Madron   A394   Pendennis Point
wall St Just A3071   Trengwainton   Relubbus   Seworgan   Port
PENWITH   Gardens   Penzance   Marazion   Wendron   Navas
A30   Newlyn   A394   Helston   Mawnan
Sennen   St Buryan   ST MICHAEL'S   Manaccan
LAND'S   Mousehole   MOUNT   Porthallow
END   6   Porthleven   Tregidden
Treen   Lamorna   A3083   St Keverne
Portho-   Porthcurno   THE LIZARD
warra St Levan   Mullion   Coverack
Mullion Cove   Penhale
Bodmin
St Austell
Carrick Roads

Colourful façade of the Egyptian House

ashes, the town was again set back by the Civil War (1642–46). It was also fair game for pirates during the 17th and 18th centuries. Charles II gave it the privilege of coining tin, but only in Victorian times did it assume its present character.

TOURING THE TOWN

From the east, past the station and inland from the large Wharfside Shopping Centre, opposite the harbour, the main thoroughfare, **Market Jew Street**, climbs to the town centre and the grandiose, granite Market House (1836). A statue of Sir Humphry Davy, born nearby in 1778, tempts seagulls. The hand of his statue rests on the miners' safety lamp that bears his name.

There are handsome 18th- and early 19th-century buildings in **Chapel Street**, which runs left from the Market House. In Princes Street stands ★★**The Exchange ❶** (open Mon–Sat 10am–5pm, Sun 11am–4pm), a stunning new art gallery with an undulating glass facade. The **Egyptian House ❷**, a vividly coloured exercise in Egyptian style, built in 1838, now houses gift shops. Further down the street, **St Mary's Church ❸** commands the harbour from a peaceful graveyard.

CORNISH PAINTERS

Close by are **Morrab Gardens** where sub-tropical plants flourish. Wander through and you emerge in Morrab Road, a quiet street lined with guest houses. At the far end is Penlee Park with a walled memorial garden and the stylishly refurbished ★**Penlee House Gallery and Museum ❹**

Map:

St Just, Land's End
Alverton Road
Penalverne Drive
St Clare Street
Coombe Road
Penlee Park
Penlee House Gallery and Museum ❹
Library
Clarence St
Alverton St
Causeway Head
High Street
Bedravia St
Jennings Road
St James St
Alma Terrace
Leskinnick Terrace
St Ives, Falmouth
Morrab Road
Morrab Gardens
The Exchange ❶
Market Jew St
Street
Railway Station
W. Promenade Rd
Queen St
Regent Sq.
❷ Egyptian House
Chapel St
Wharf Road
Bus Station
Newlyn
St Mary's Church ❸
Harbour
❺ Trinity House National Lighthouse Centre
Battery Rd
The Quay
South Pier
Dock
Jubilee Bathing Pool

PENZANCE

0 — 400 m
0 — 400 yards

(open Easter–Sept: Mon–Sat 10am–5pm; Oct–Easter: 10.30am–4.30pm). It is well worth a visit to see many of the works of the Newlyn School painters (*see page 77*).

Back on the seafront, a left turn along the broad promenade takes you to the art deco **Jubilee Bathing Pool** (open May–Sept; times vary), inaugurated in 1935 for the Silver Jubilee of George V. A little further along, in Wharf Road, the Old Buoy Store contains the **Trinity House National Lighthouse Centre ❺** (open Easter– Oct: daily 10am–4.30pm), dedicated to safety at sea.

ST MICHAEL'S MOUNT

The rocky island of ★★★ **St Michael's Mount** looms across the bay and, inevitably, comparison is made with Mont St Michel in Normandy. There is more than a visual connection: King Edward the Confessor granted the Mount to the Benedictine monks of St Michel and, by 1140, they had founded a church there. With Henry VIII's Dissolution of the Monasteries in the 1530s, the Crown installed a governor and fortified the buildings. In the Civil War the Roundheads laid siege to the Mount, which fell after a long struggle.

Afterwards, Colonel John St Aubyn, put in charge by the Parliamentarians, bought the island. More than three centuries later, the St Aubyn family still live in the **castle** (NT; open Easter–Oct: Sun–Fri 10.30am–5.30pm; tel: 01736-710507 for information and tours in winter; all visits depend on weather conditions). The Mount is reached by a cobbled causeway at low tide, by ferry when the tide is high. Anyone can walk across when the tide is low, as long as they give themselves time to walk back; the hours above refer just to the castle.

The approach to the castle's Tudor doorway from the Causeway is made via the pier, the harbour, the estate village and 200 Pilgrims' Steps. The **Chevy Chase Room**, which was the monks' refectory, is a medieval survivor, with a later (17th-century) plaster frieze depicting hunting scenes. The **Blue Drawing Rooms** are decorated in Georgian rococo-Gothic style.

Star Attraction
● St Michael's Mount

News from Trafalgar
The company in the Assembly Rooms of the Union Hotel, in Penzance's Chapel Street, were the first to receive news in 1815 of Admiral Horatio Nelson's victory, and his death, at Trafalgar.

St Michael's Mount

Map on page 47

★ **Marazion**, at the terrestrial end of the causeway, was granted an early charter, in 1257. It became an important market town – the pronunciation of Maghas Yow – Thursday Market – has blurred over the years to Marazion. The old fire station is now a **Museum** (open May–Oct: Mon–Sat, and Sun in Jul–Aug) and the Cornish painter, Michael Praed, has a gallery here.

ANCIENT CORNWALL

Draw a line from Mount's Bay to St Ives Bay and what is left of Cornwall is **West Penwith**. In Cornish, *penwyth* means farthest end. It was here that the Cornish language survived longest, with its last speaker living at Mousehole. A walk in the granite uplands produces convincing evidence that the area was densely inhabited in prehistoric times: past civilisations have their memorials in standing stones, fortified castles, village clusters, burial chambers and stone circles on the heather-covered moors.

Below: ancient stones
Bottom: boats at Newlyn

Leaving Penzance along the promenade, the first building on the left (in New Road) when you reach **Newlyn** is the large, light space of the ★★**Newlyn Gallery** (open Mon–Sat 10am–5pm, Sun 11am–4pm), newly renovated and extended to form a glass pavilion. It features the work of artists of regional, national and international importance, and introduces Newlyn as the home of one of Britain's leading art colonies. Here, Stanhope Forbes, Norman Garstin, 'Lamorna' Birch and others set up easels and sent their paintings to the Royal Academy in London. But pretty little Newlyn is not all about art: it has a thriving fishing industry as well.

From Newlyn, the B3315, the A30 and the Penzance by-pass lead to Heamoor and then to ★**Trengwainton Garden** (NT; open mid-Feb–Oct: Sun–Thurs 10am–5pm). In five intimate walled gardens semi-tropical and tender plants, not found elsewhere in mainland Britain, are grown outdoors. Views over Mount's Bay are shared with **Madron**. Here, in the church of St Maddern's, the Trafalgar Banner commemorates the news of Nelson's death. In the workhouse, naïve painter Alfred Wallis died in 1942. The 14th-century **Holy Well**, a mile above the village, was credited with healing powers by a 17th-century Bishop of Exeter.

Star Attraction
● Mousehole

MOUSEHOLE AND LAMORNA

Downhill from Newlyn Bridge crossroads is ★★ **Mousehole** (pronounced *Mowzel*), the archetypal Cornish fishing village. Guests are accommodated in granite cottages in the alleys and courtyards on the hill above. Only one house survived the 1595 Spanish raid, the old Keigwin Arms, an Elizabethan manor distinguished by a porch on granite columns.

Continue along the B3315, and after about a mile, turn left at Trewoofe to run alongside a trout stream down the delightful ★ **Lamorna Valley**. A few cottages, an old mill and an inn called The Wink are the setting for a summer idyll. Granite from the quarry was shipped at ★ **Lamorna Cove** to build London's Thames Embankment.

> **Tragedy in Mousehole**
> The small community of Mousehole was devastated in December 1981 by the loss of their lifeboat, the *Solomon Browne*, with all eight of its crew. The boat was launched in a hurricane-force gale in a courageous attempt to rescue the crew of the *Union Star* aground on the rocks near Lamorna.

MERRY MAIDENS TO MINACK

A mile or so along the B3315 is the Bronze Age ceremonial site, the Merry Maidens (*see page 9*). The road soon leads to the village of Treen. From

Porthcurno's idyllic bay, beside Minack Theatre

Map on page 47

a car park, **★ Logan Rock**, a huge boulder situated on the crest of the spectacular headland of Treryn Dinas, can be reached by a footpath.

At nearby **Porthcurno** is a beautiful beach of golden sand. Just behind the beach is the fascinating **★ Museum of Submarine Technology** (open Apr–Oct: Sun–Fri 10am–5pm; Nov–Mar: Sun & Mon 10am–5pm). The museum is housed in World War II fortified tunnels in the cliff.

Summer brings actors to Porthcurno and the **★★ Minack Theatre** (visits: Apr–Sept: daily 9.30am–5.30pm; Oct–Mar: 10am–4pm; tel: 01736-810181 for information about afternoon closures on performance days and tickets for performances). This cliff-edge amphitheatre was constructed by the remarkable Rowena Cade, beginning in the 1930s. The whole glorious endeavour is explored in the **Exhibition Centre**.

Ancient relics

By turning right at Morvah, just past the Geevor Tin Mine on the road to Madron and Penzance, some of the moorland's most interesting relics can be reached. There is Chun Castle, an Iron Age fort; Chun Cromlech, a chamber tomb; Lanyon Quoit; and the oldest — possibly Roman — mine, the Ding Dong.

From Zennor, the Neolithic Zennor Quoit, unique in that it covers two tombs, and Giant's Rock, a logan stone on the hill above the church, are both invitingly close.

LAND'S END

The B3315 joins the A30 for **★ Land's End**, England's most westerly point. There is nothing except the Isles of Scilly between here and America. The Romans called Land's End *Belerion*, meaning the 'seat of storms'. Today it's described as a 'multi-attraction', and offers a highly commercialised experience in the **Land's End Centre** (open daily 10am–5pm; tel: 01736-871501), a complex that

Minack Theatre has a stunning setting

embraces a hotel, cafés, a multi-sensory theatre, birdwatching, crafts and a beached 54-ton trawler.

As you leave on the Penzance road, **Sennen**, England's westernmost village, promises hospitality at the First and Last Inn. Tiny ★ **Sennen Cove**, tucked in under the hill at the western end of Whitesand Bay surfing beach, has pretty thatched cottages and a showcase for modern crafts in the former capstan house.

ST JUST TO ZENNOR

Branching left from the Penzance road, the B3306 soon passes an airfield from which you can fly to the Isles of Scilly *(see page 90)*, and then enters **St Just**, capital of an industry that died with the fall in the price of tin. With the predominance of granite and slate the town looks rather severe, but it's a friendly place. 'Plen-an-Gwary', the **Playing Place**, was a medieval spot that attracted crowds to miracle plays. Cape Cornwall Street leads to ★ **Cape Cornwall**, crowned with a monumental mine chimney. England's only cape looks to the vicious teeth of the Brisons rocks.

The rugged coast near Zennor

The coast road traverses an area once mined intensively for tin and copper. The Crown's Mine at **Botallack** has the most picturesque of the old mine buildings, with engine houses perched precariously on the cliff. The restored ★ **Levant Beam Engine** (NT; diverse opening hours; tel: 01736-786156) is the oldest working beam engine in Cornwall. Half a mile (1 km) along the cliff is ★ **Geevor Tin Mine Museum** (not NT; open Apr–Oct: Sun–Fri 9am–5pm; Nov–Mar: till 4pm; last visit and underground tour, an hour before closing; tel: 01736-788662).

Continuing on the B3306, a church tower signals a chapel, inn and little group of granite dwellings, set among fields strewn with enormous boulders. This is ★ **Zennor**, where a legendary mermaid lured a chorister beneath the waves after falling in love with his voice. The fascinating **Wayside Folk Museum** (open Apr–Oct: daily 10.30am–5.30pm) traces Zennor's history with a wealth of domestic and rural treasures.

Map
on page
55

7: The Isles of Scilly

St Mary's – Tresco – Bryher – St Agnes – St Martin's

There are few places in Britain where the air is so clear, the water such a vivid blue, or the pace of life so tranquil as the Isles of Scilly, a small cluster of islands 28 miles (45 km) southwest of Land's End. They comprise five inhabited islands, with a total population of around 2,000, and over 100 smaller islands. They are tiny – the largest, St Mary's, is barely 3 miles (5 km) at its widest point. A mild climate means tropical plants and bulbs thrive; together with tourism these form the mainstay of the economy, although the flower industry is declining. The islands can be equally magical when the weather turns bad. In winter they face the full force of the Atlantic. For details of how to get here, by sea or air, *see page 90*.

MYTH AND REALITY

Steeped in myth and legend, the islands have been associated with the Arthurian Lyonesse, the Atlantis of the Greeks and the Cassiterides (tin islands) of the Phoenicians. What is certain is that they have been inhabited for at least 4,000 years, as countless Bronze Age burial mounds testify.

Below: exotic flowers bloom on the islands
Bottom: calm, safe waters

For much of their history, the islanders had to scratch a living from anything the sea had to offer, including shipwrecks. Prosperity only arrived in 1834 when Augustus Smith obtained the lease of the islands from the Duchy of Cornwall, and became Lord Proprietor. He introduced social reforms and encouraged shipbuilding.

Star Attraction
● Isles of Scilly Museum

St Mary's

Shipyards once occupied the beach adjacent to the quayside at **St Mary's**, the first port of call for visitors arriving by sea. It is only a short walk into the Scillies' main town, **Hugh Town**, which straddles the island at its narrowest point. You could visit the **Mermaid** pub before continuing up the road on the right, through the **Garrison Gate** to **Star Castle**. Now a hotel, the castle was built in 1593 as protection against pirates and possible invasion by the Spanish. In 1646, during the Civil War, the castle was a refuge for the Prince of Wales (Charles II) and his retinue after their defeat at Bodmin. It was secured by the Parliamentarians after their victory at Tresco in 1651.

Gig races
The gigs in the Isles of Scilly Museum can be seen in action by summer visitors; they race between the Tresco Channel and St Mary's every Wednesday and Friday evening in the gig races.

Scilly Isles ferry

Isles of Scilly Museum

Continue through Hugh Town into Church Road, where the ★★ **Isles of Scilly Museum** (open Apr: Mon–Sat 10am–noon, 1.30–4.30pm; May–Sept: 7.30–9pm; Nov–Feb: Wed 2–4pm) offers an insight into life on the islands. Exhibits range from Bronze and Iron Age artefacts to remnants of shipwrecks, including the worst single disaster in British naval history when four ships under the command of Sir Cloudesley Shovell were wrecked on the Western Rocks in 1707, with the loss of over 1,400 men. The museum's centrepiece is a restored pilot boat (gig).

This fascinating museum also has a natural history section highlighting species that live here for at least part of the year. The puffin and the Atlantic seal are popular residents of the Western Rocks.

Map on page 55

St Mary's has some magnificent coastline, nowhere more than at ★ **Penninis Head** on the south coast. There is also much evidence of ancient history on the island, including ★ **Bant's Carn Burial Chamber**.

Uninhabited islands
Between Tresco and St Martin's are the uninhabited islands of Tean, once used for cattle grazing and the production of kelp ash; and St Helen's, where the remains of the oldest Christian building on the islands are to be found.

Tresco Abbey Gardens

TRESCO

Depending on the tide, visitors to the paradise island of **Tresco** usually arrive at **New Grimsby** harbour. A long promenade leads around the harbour, where the road turns left up hill to Old Grimsby. Most visitors continue straight on, following signs to ★★★ **Tresco Abbey Gardens** (open all year: daily 10am–4pm). Laid out in the 19th century by Augustus Smith on the site of the Benedictine Priory of St Nicholas, the gardens were enlarged and improved by successive members of his family, and contain rare plants from all over the Southern Hemisphere, especially south Africa and Mexico, many brought back to the islands by ships' captains. In the gardens is the **Figurehead Valhalla**, a museum of figureheads culled from shipwrecks.

The southern end of Tresco is flanked by beautiful, empty beaches. Continue along the east coast past Pentle Bay and the old Blockhouse to **Old Grimsby**, from where it is possible to explore the rugged northern end of the island, whose features include **Pipers' Hole**, a cave with a small underground lake. On the west coast the most distinctive man-made feature is the tower of ★ **Cromwell's Castle**, built on the promontory beneath the older King Charles' Castle in 1651.

BRYHER

Just opposite Tresco is **Bryher**, the smallest of the five inhabited islands, with a permanent population of under 100. An island of contrasts, its interior offers a rural idyll of patchwork fields and downs, while the rocky west coast is dramatic. The settled part of the island starts at the **church** by the main quay and winds uphill, dropping down to the coast once more at the general store, the post office and the **Fraggle Rock Café**. A path leads up to the northern tip, offering beautiful walks over the downs. The rocky headland of ★ **Shipman Head** is separated from the island by a narrow cleft, so having visited **Hell Bay**, which even on a day of moderate swell offers spectacular views of the sea lashing against the rocks, walkers can continue down the west coast.

The most beautiful feature at the island's southern end is **Rushy Bay**, overlooking uninhabited **Samson** island. Behind the bay is **Samson Hill** from where there are magnificent views.

Star Attraction
● Tresco Abbey Gardens

ST AGNES AND ST MARTIN'S

St Agnes is the most southwesterly community in the British Isles. Principal industries are fishing and flower growing. The deeply indented coastline and heath downs support a profusion of wild flowers and butterflies.

At low tide you can walk across a sandbar to the small island of ★ **Gugh**. Near the main jetty is the Turk's Head, renowned for good food and fine views. In the centre of the island, and visible from afar, is a disused, 17th-century, coal-burning lighthouse. An even more striking feature, the red and white striped Day Mark, dominates the easternmost inhabited island of **St Martin's**, popular for its magnificent beaches.

Below: craggy rocks of Bryher
Bottom: Cromwell's Castle

Map
on page
47

8: Art and Industry

St Ives – Camborne – St Agnes

The twisting road from Zennor skirts the hills and enters ★★★ **St Ives**, the most lively and interesting of all Cornwall's resorts; the road passes Higher Stennack and the ★**Leach Studio Pottery**, established in 1920 by the late Bernard Leach. Examples of his work are exhibited here, along with that of other potters. The pottery was recently saved from closure and substantially refurbished; it is due to re-open in Spring 2008.

UPALONG AND DOWNALONG

The most distinguished physical feature of St Ives is 'The Island', which divides the Atlantic surfing beach of Porthmeor from the harbour and from the smaller beach of Porthminster. At the highest point is the little granite chapel of St Nicholas, on the site of one built by St Ia in the 6th century on her arrival from Ireland.

Pilchards made St Ives prosperous. Houses were built with fish processing in mind. Salting and packing in barrels for export took place in the cellars below the living quarters, reached by steps to the first floor, which are still commonly seen in the tangle of narrow streets near the harbour.

Alfred Wallis

Reproductions of the work of the semi-literate primitive painter, Alfred Wallis, who took up painting at the age of 70 after life as a seaman and a rag-and-bone merchant, can be seen all over St Ives. His remarkable images of ships, fishing boats and St Ives scenes were painted on old pieces of wood, on cardboard and on whatever came to hand. Although 'discovered' by Ben Nicholson and Christopher Wood in the 1930s, he died penniless before his works received the recognition accorded to them today.

St Ives is good for families as well as artists

This was 'Downalong', home of the fishing community. Higher up the town lived the miners, in the area called 'Upalong'.

Both suffered economic disaster, the fishermen with the disappearance of pilchards and the miners with the collapse of the tin market. Survival came from an unexpected quarter: the unique quality of the light and the appeal of the subject matter attracted artists. Fish cellars and net lofts were converted into studios and into accommodation for the growing holiday industry.

THE TATE

Cornwall has its own major art gallery in the ★★★ **Tate St Ives** (open Mar–Oct: daily 10am–5.20pm; Nov–Feb: Tues–Sun 10am–4.20pm). The gallery holds only a small permanent collection of works by St Ives painters such as Ben Nicholson, Peter Lanyon, Patrick Heron, Sir Terry Frost and others, but presents changing displays from the Tate Collection of modern art, concentrating on works connected with Cornwall; and temporary exhibitions of works by other artists. The building is a delight in itself, as is its position, opposite Porthmeor beach. The view from the restaurant and upper terrace is like a spectacular painting in its own right.

Tate St Ives offers a splendid setting for works of art

An integral part of the Tate is the ★★ **Barbara Hepworth Museum** (hours as for the Tate; combined tickets available) in Trewyn Studio on Barnoon Hill. Hepworth's vital spirit is much in evidence in her studio and sculpture garden.

Close by, the **Wills Lane Gallery** (open Mon–Sat 10.30am–5pm) shows the works of Alfred Wallis, Ben Nicholson, Christopher Wood, and many of today's artists. The **St Ives Society of Artists** (founded 1927), exhibits excellent works in the **Norway Gallery** (open late Mar–Nov: Mon–Sat 10am–4.30pm), in the the light, airy nave of the old Mariners' Church in Norway Square, behind the Sloop Inn. The **Mariners' Gallery** in the crypt also has special exhibitions).

In 1949 a splinter group of modern artists formed the **Penwith Society of Arts**, which

Map
on page
47

exhibits at the **Penwith Gallery** (open Tues–Sat, 10am–1pm, 2.30–5pm) in Back Road West. The **New Millennium Gallery** (open Mar–Oct: Mon–Sat 10.30am–4.30pm; Nov–Dec: Fri–Sat & Mon) on Street-an-Pol shows the work of contemporary artists. Local characters have their gallery in the popular **Sloop Inn**. In the appealing **St Ives Museum** (open Easter, May–Oct: Mon–Fri 10am–5pm, Sat 10am–4pm) you can learn about the history of St Ives and its people.

The tall granite tower of the 15th-century church of **St Ia** impresses most from the sea. Inside are barrel roofs, bench-ends, columns carved with grapes and vine leaves, and Barbara Hepworth's 1954 *Madonna and Child*.

Proud resident of Paradise Park

CARBIS BAY AND PARADISE PARK

The A3074 climbs above St Ives' railway station, with panoramic backward views over the town, and passes through Carbis Bay where a diversion left leads to the superb Carbis Bay beach. At **Lelant**, a golf course and church share the sandhills of the Hayle estuary, and West Penwith is left behind at Quay House, the birdwatchers' hide at the head of the saltings. Further on, at Hayle, is ★★ **Paradise Park** (open all year: daily from 10am; last admission 5pm summer, 3pm winter), home of the World Parrot Trust, where there is a superb collection of rare birds and other creatures; otter and penguin feeding times are popular.

HAYLE TO GODREVY LIGHTHOUSE

East of St Ives is the heart of Cornwall's once thriving mining industry. **Hayle** makes an appropriate introduction because the great beam engines were made here. In **Millpond Gardens**, the foundry's ruins have been laid out as a park round the hammer mill and pond. The road follows the canal through **Copperhouse**, which lost its tin and copper smelting to Swansea. Left at the crossroads beyond, the B3301 passes the *towans* (sandhills), with splendid views of St Ives across the bay, until **Gwithian** is reached. The little group of thatched cottages, a church and an inn have a timeless air. What may be England's oldest Christian building, St Gothian's Chapel, was discovered buried in the sand beside the Red River – the mine waste turned the water red.

Just offshore is ★ **Godrevy Lighthouse**, the inspiration for Virginia Woolf's 1927 novel *To the Lighthouse*, and beyond is Navax Point, a breeding-place for seals. The slate cliffs here open to frightening chasms in Hell's Mouth and Deadman's Cove. A road forks right from the coast and right again to regain the A30 outside Camborne.

MINES AND ENGINES

At the end of April **Camborne** honours Richard Trevithick, 'Father of the Locomotive'. His statue outside the Library on Trevenson Street clutches a model of his steam locomotive, which anticipated Stephenson's Rocket by 12 years, but it was for his high-pressure steam-pumping engine that Camborne has most to thank him. At the Library you can get information about the Great Flat Lode Trail and Coast to Coast Trail, part of the **Mineral Tramways Heritage Project**, that have recently been opened up to walkers and cyclists (tel: 01872-222000). There is little else to see here: Camborne is a town that lost its industry and gained few tourists, and the poverty is obvious.

Star Attraction
● Paradise Park

Tin mining

Towards the end of the 18th century the problem of keeping water out of Cornwall's mines had become pressing, and began to attract the attention of engineers; first came James Watt with his steam pumping engine, then Richard Trevithick, who improved on Watt's invention and designed steam-powered engines to crush the ore.

Buildings and chimneys began to appear in their hundreds around Camborne and Redruth, and by 1850 nearly three-quarters of the world's copper and half its tin came from Cornwall.

Godrevy Lighthouse inspired Virginia Woolf

Map on page 47

At **Pool**, on the road to Redruth, just outside town, the ★ **Cornish Engines** (NT; open Apr–Oct: Sun–Mon, Wed–Fri 11am–5pm; Nov–Mar: by arrangement, tel: 01209-315027) can be seen, lovingly restored and working smoothly. The first is visible on the right; the other, larger engine and an abandoned mine complex incorporate an audio-visual presentation in the **Industrial Discovery Centre**, tucked behind Safeway's car park to the left.

Crowning glory
Visible from the Cornish Pumping engines site is the 90-ft (27-metre) monument erected in 1837 to Francis Basset, Lord de Dunstanville, mine- and landowner. It is accessible from the crossroads at Poole's Station Road, where there are signs to Carnkie. A lane on the left climbs to the summit of the distinctive hill of Carn Brea, site of human activity since prehistoric times. The monument overlooks the remains of the once highly productive Basset mines.

REDRUTH

Turn right off the A30 onto the A393 for **Redruth**. The area around light, airy **St Euny**'s church is a pleasant, leafy corner in a hard industrial landscape. It still has a 15th-century tower and a lych gate with unusually long granite slabs on which coffins rested after mining disasters. The Scotsman William Murdock is Redruth's revered celebrity: a prolific inventor, his best-known achievement is gas lighting. His was the first house to be lit by gas, and the light still burns in Cross Street near the bottom of Fore Street.

PORTREATH

Cornish Engines, protected by the National Trust

Francis Basset (*see box*) created **Portreath** – reached from Redruth by the B3300 – because

there was no suitable port from which to ship ore and import Welsh coal and timber. The harbour, constructed in 1760, was superseded in the early 1800s by a more ambitious one with two inner docks. It was served by Cornwall's first railway, with wagons lowered to the quay from the hill above by an engine at the top. The little town has a fine beach and is popular for family holidays. It is also the starting point of the **Coast to Coast Trail**, part of the Mineral Tramways project (look out for the trail waymark near the Portreath Arms). Cycles can be hired in Redruth and Bissoe *(see pages 61 and 88)*.

Returning to Redruth, the A393 leads in 2 miles (3 km) to Gwennap and the scene of some of John Wesley's greatest gatherings. At ★ **Gwennap Pit** he once addressed a congregation of 30,000.

Star Attraction
● **St Agnes**

ST AGNES

At Scorrier take the A30 towards Newquay, then go left on the B3277 to reach friendly little ★★ **St Agnes**. The village, the cliffs and 600-ft (180-metre), heather-clad St Agnes Beacon all show signs of a mining past. Mining, fishing and folklore take precedence in the ★ **St Agnes Museum** (open Easter–Oct: daily 10.30am–5pm) in Penwinnick Road, but the prize exhibit is a giant leatherback turtle, washed ashore in 1988.

A hotel, an inn, a pretty church and a few small galleries mark the turn downhill past a terrace of miners' cottages known as Stippy Stappy, to Quay Road and the town's port at **Trevaunance Cove**. This idyllic little spot, much loved by surfers, has a small beach and a ceramics gallery next to the 17th-century Driftwood Inn.

At Trevellas Coombe, to the north, you can visit **Blue Hills Tin Streams** (open Mar–Oct: Mon–Sat 10.30am–5pm) where you can watch the process of extracting and smelting tin and buy some of the finished products. Also in Trevellas stands the thatched **Harmony Cot**, where John Opie, the 'Cornish Wonder' *(see page 77)*, was born in 1761. He became a fashionable portrait painter and is buried in St Paul's Cathedral.

St Agnes lifeguard ready for action

Map
below

9: The North Coast Resorts

Perranporth – Newquay – Padstow

Holidaymakers have made a big impression on this coast. Seaside bungalows have invaded much of the coastline not snatched to safety by the National Trust. Caravans have taken possession of coves, sands are the province of surfers, and golfers drive off from some of the best views. Yet natural attractions assert their pulling power, and it is still possible to find tranquillity.

Perranporth, first stop on this stretch of coast, can be reached along the winding B3285 from St Agnes. It is, undeniably, a shabby little place, but surfers find all they need here *(see page 88)*, and the great stretch of **Perran Sands** is popular with families.

Passing Perranporth Golf Course and several caravan sites, the B3285 joins the A3075 at Goonhavern and heads towards Newquay.

Change of name

Newquay began as Towan Blystra, a fishing cove which acquired a new name when a Newe Kaye was built in Elizabethan times. Another new quay was constructed in 1838 so that china clay from St Austell could be shipped from here. The arrival of the railway 40 years later brought the tourists, and the Great Western Hotel in the town centre, and the splendid Atlantic and Headland hotels that still stand on the cliff tops, were built in order to accommodate them.

ROUTE 9

0   5 km
0   5 miles

NEWQUAY

★ **Newquay** is the biggest and brashest resort on the coast and a magnet for serious surfers *(see page 88)*. From the south, the road into town crosses the head of the Gannel estuary, and leads to **Fistral Bay**, the biggest of the town's three beaches, and the one where the major surfing championships are held. Budget hotels and B&Bs, with wetsuits drying at the windows, line the streets as you approach the beach.

Turning right towards the town centre, you must follow the one-way system. Close to Fore Street is the pretty harbour, and some of the town's oldest houses poised above a sheer cliff face. A road (and a flight of steps) spiral down to the quays, where there's a sandy beach at low tide.

FAMILY ENTERTAINMENT

Newquay is crammed with amusement arcades and fast-food joints, and also has a wealth of family entertainment. In St Michael's Road, in the town centre, **Tunnels Through Time** (open Easter–Oct: Sun–Fri 10am–4pm, mid-Jul–Aug: daily) brings Cornish legends and history to life with life-size figures in imaginative settings. The **Blue Reef Aquarium** (open daily from 10am; last admission 4pm) on Towan Promenade, is informative and entertaining, and holds fish feeding demonstrations. **Newquay Zoo** (open Apr–Oct: daily 9.30am–6pm, Nov–Mar: 10am–dusk) at Trenance, off Edgcumbe Avenue, Cornwall's only zoo, places emphasis on efforts to save animals through captive breeding.

Below: making the most of the Atlantic surf and (bottom) broad stretches of sand

CHANGE OF PACE

At Kestle Mill on the A392 from Newquay, signs point to ★★★ **Trerice** (NT; house open mid-Mar–Oct: Sun–Fri 11am–5pm; gardens 10.30am–5pm). Of all Cornwall's country houses, this glorious Elizabethan manor is the most

Below: Trerice
Bottom: a slate wall, locally
known as a 'curzyway'

exquisitely furnished and decorated. It was rebuilt in 1571 on the site of an older house, by Sir John Arundell. The window that lights the Great Hall, rising through two storeys, has 576 panes of glass. The oak table, 20 ft (6 metres) long, was specially made in the early 19th century. The gardens, with some rare perennials, shrubs and climbers, are quite gorgeous.

A return to Kestle Mill and the fringes of Newquay leads to a drive along the A3059, past St Mawgan Airfield to **St Columb Major**. The church, with a broad, 14th-century nave and delicate rood screen and reredos (a 20th-century restoration) was shortlisted for elevation to cathedral status, but Truro won by a short head. It is a peaceful village, with a couple of antique shops and a 16th-century tea room serving coffee that alone would make the detour worthwhile.

THE VALE OF LANHERNE

Back on the A3059, a first right turn running through woods of the Vale of Lanherne descends to **St Mawgan** and the Falcon Inn. Old stone bridges and a ford cross the stream to the village, but through the lych gate there is an inviting path to the church, where the Arundell brasses are the most significant objects. Beyond the wall opposite the church door is **Lanherne**, which has been the seat of the Arundell family since 1231.

Up the steps is a 15th-century lantern cross and, higher up, a memorial to nine men and a boy washed ashore frozen to death in 1846. The road and a path pass the house, which incorporates part of the Elizabethan building. In 1794 a party of English Carmelite nuns fleeing from the French Revolution were offered sanctuary by Lord Arundell, and it is still used as a convent today. **Lanherne Chapel** is open to the public.

COASTAL DIVERSIONS

The hill across the stream and a left-hand turn at the top follows the Vale down to **Mawgan Porth**, where evidence of a 10th-century village coexists with a 21st-century holiday camp. Northwards, the cliff road climbs to ★ **Bedruthan Steps**, rocks rising from the sand that were, according to legend, the giant Bedruthan's stepping stones. **Porthcothan**, where cliffs with caves and arches are protected by the National Trust, begins a series of bathing beaches: **Treyarnon, Constantine, Mother Ivey's Bay** and **Harlyn**, all accessible from the B3276. Harlyn made headlines in 1990 when workmen digging foundations of a house uncovered a Celtic burial ground.

From the road to Trevose Head, the ruins of the 14th-century chapel of **St Constantine** can be seen in the golf course. Beyond that, the **Lighthouse** and the rocky headland of Trevose can be seen. Tucked into its lee on Mother Ivey's Bay is the Padstow Lifeboat Station.

Star Attraction
● Padstow

Birds of prey
On the A39 at Winnards Perch, between St Columb Major and Wadebridge, is the Cornish Birds of Prey Centre (tel: 01637 880544). There are deer, ponies and peacocks too, and coarse fishing is available. Displays are usually held at noon and 2.30pm.

PADSTOW AND PRIDEAUX PLACE

★★★ **Padstow** lies up the estuary beyond the Doom Bar, the sandbank that wrecked many a ship attempting to reach harbour in stormy conditions. The Bar and a silted-up estuary have plagued Padstow for centuries, but it still sustains a small fishing fleet. Old stone and slate cottages, slate-hung inns and warehouses make an attractive setting, with cobbled byways and streets climbing a valley to the church of St Petroc.

Padstow's harbour is pretty by night or day

Map on page 64

Myths and legends

Padstow has long been a place of legend and myth. It is said that the treacherous Doom Bar sandbank was caused by a mermaid throwing sand – and a curse – at a man who had attacked her.

Another legend attaches to the font in St Petroc's church: legend has it that anyone baptised there could never be hanged. However, when a local man was caught robbing the mail and paid the usual penalty, that myth was confounded.

The church sits below the grounds of ★★ **Prideaux Place** (open Easter, May–Sept: Sun–Thur 1.30–5pm, last tour 4pm; grounds: 12.30–5pm), located to the left of the B3276 as you enter Padstow. Home of the Prideaux-Brune family since it was built in 1592, the richly furnished Elizabethan manor overlooks its own deer park, the town and the estuary. Looking just the way an English stately home is supposed to look, it has often been used as a location for films.

The embossed ceiling of its Great Chamber tells the biblical story of Susannah and the Elders, and the Library is a delightful exercise in Georgian Gothic. There are woodland walks in the grounds and a restored formal garden. In the church of **St Petroc** just below is a wall monument to Sir Nicholas Prideaux (1624), and on a bench-end, a fox preaches to geese.

THE TOWN AND THE QUAY

Down on the quay, lesser mortals enjoy themselves admiring the harbour views and frequenting the small shops, cafés and restaurants that cater to all tastes and pockets (for the Rick Stein phenomenon, *see page 86*). On North Quay, ancient **Abbey House** is believed to have been the site of a chapel. From the slipway here, beside the tourist office, the Black Tor ferry runs across the estuary to Rock (daily except Sun in Nov–Mar) and there are water taxis at night.

On South Quay is Sir Walter Raleigh's Courthouse in a 16th-century building. Nearby, the stuccoed front of the Custom House is obscured by an extension to the Custom House Inn.

In Market Place, ★ **Padstow Museum** (open Apr–Oct: Mon–Fri 10.30am–4.30pm, Sat 10.30am–1pm, but times may vary) has displays on lifeboats, on schooners and shipwrecks, and on the railway that came and went. It also has a genuine 'Obby Oss' and old photos of May Day celebrations. However, the museum has to leave these premises in June 2005 and is currently seeking a new home. Just off Market Place is the tiny Cinedrome, which has been a cinema since 1924.

Rick Stein – the master at work in his kitchen

10: The Atlantic Highway

Wadebridge – Port Isaac – Camelford – Tintagel – Boscastle – Morwenstow

Map on page 70

The Atlantic Highway, a rather grand name for the unassuming A39, parallels Cornwall's north coast from the River Camel to Devon's Welcombe, but at a respectful distance. The coast is wild, untameable and, for those at sea, downright dangerous. Churchyards groan with mariners pulled dead from the sea, caught by an on-shore wind and a rising tide with 3,000 miles (4,800 km) of Atlantic behind it. Harbours are small and inhospitable, supporting very modest fishing. Roads approach down precipitous hills. Railways shun it altogether. Yet it is much loved: romantics flock to Tintagel in search of King Arthur, to Morwenstow in homage to the Reverend Hawker, and to Boscastle where Thomas Hardy (1840–1928) found his first love *(see pages 80–81)*.

Star Attraction
● Prideaux Place

WADEBRIDGE AND THE CAMEL TRAIL

From Padstow, the A389 dips down to pretty **Little Petherick**, with an ancient stone bridge and church, at the head of the creek. Shortly, a right turn from the bypass descends to **Wadebridge**. A steam railway, the first in Cornwall and second

Below: bikes to ride on the Camel Trail
Bottom: the sturdy stone bridge at Wadebridge

Map below

Honouring a much-loved poet

in England, linked Bodmin with Wadebridge in 1834, and in 1899 a branch to Padstow was opened. The tracks have gone, but the **Camel Trail** for walkers and cyclists has replaced them. Wadebridge Station now houses the ★ **John Betjeman Centre** (open Mon–Fri 10am–4pm) celebrating the much-loved Poet Laureate (1906–84).

There is a flower-hung inn, terraced cottages with pretty porches, and council houses crowding behind. ★ **Egloshayle** church has a fine stone tower, built by Thomas Lovibond, vicar of Egloshayle, in about 1485. He also built the magnificent stone bridge across the Camel.

ROCK, RUMPS AND PORT QUIN

Rock, signposted off the A39 above the bridge, has been connected by ferry to Padstow since the 14th century, and still is today *(see page 68)*. Paths climb the 'Himalayas', the sand dunes, and cross the golf course to the church of ★ **St Enedoc**, which was buried in sand until 1863. Inside the church is Sir John Betjeman's favourite pew, and in the churchyard a slate headstone marks where he was buried in 1984. The family's holiday home was at Trebetherick nearby.

Just beyond Polzeath is the ★ **Rumps**, an Iron Age hill fort on a headland that's almost an island, defended by ditches and ramparts. Inside are traces of the round huts of the original inhabitants. Parking, courtesy of the National Trust, is at Pentire Farm.

Left from the road east of Pentire is the tiny fishing cove of ★ **Port Quin**, overlooked by the cliff-top folly of Doyden Castle.

ROUTE 10

0 — 8 km
0 — 8 miles

Morwenstow
Higher Sharpnose Pt
Lower Sharpnose Pt
Coombe
Stibb
Bideford
Kilkhampton
A39
Stratton
Bude
A3072
Helebridge
Bude Bay
Poundstock
Wainhouse Corner
Week St Mary
Collamoor Head
Boscastle
A39
Hailworthy
Tintagel Head
Bossiney
Treknow
Tintagel
Trewassa
A395
Delabole
Port Isaac Bay
Crowdy R.
Rough Tor
Rumps Pt
Camelford
B O D M I N
Port Quinn
Port Isaac
Bolventor
A30
Trelights
Polzeath
M O O R
Little Petherick
A39
Blisland
Colliford Lake R.
Wadebridge
Newquay
Bodmin
Otter
Launceston

FROM TRELIGHTS TO PORT ISAAC

At **Trelights**, en route to St Endellion and behind Long Cross Hotel, is the **Long Cross Victorian Garden** (open daily 11am–dusk). A maze of paths make every turn in this 2½-acre (1-hectare) garden of shrubs and herbaceous borders a delight. And there are good cream teas. At ★ **St Endellion** on the B3314 is a church that has retained its collegiate status to the present day, with prebends' stalls, and prebends' cottages in the little settlement outside. There are rhymes on the headstones and, in the bell-ringers' tower, a 14th-century tomb chest. Waggon roofs and carved bench-ends make this one of Cornwall's finest churches.

Beside the church, a twisting lane drops down to the fishing village of ★★ **Port Isaac**, although the village proper is reached from the official car park. The lifeboat had to be manhandled down the narrow street and launched from the beach. Fish cellars, an inn, a stream and closely packed cottages make it a fascinating place to explore.

DELABOLE

Over the headland at **Port Gaverne** schooners once loaded slate from Delabole off the beach, and pilchards filled the fish cellars. The continuing road joins the B3314 (opposite the Cycle Museum) to enter a village that owes its existence

Star Attraction
● Port Isaac

> 👁 **The Camel Trail**
> The Camel Trail covers 16 miles (24 km), following the course of the old LSWR railway line, between Padstow and Blisland. Bikes can be hired for reasonable rates from Bridge Bike Hire near the Old Bridge in Wadebridge (tel: 01208-813050, open all year). They supply a rudimentary map, which also advises you about good places to stop for refreshment. You can, of course, bring your own bike, and join the trail at various points.

The north coast is stunning whatever the season

A new form of energy at Delabole Wind Farm

to a hole in the ground – the biggest man-made hole in Britain. **Delabole Slate Quarry** (open May–Sept: Mon–Fri (not BH Mon), presentations and tours at 2pm), down a short road on the right past quarrymen's cottages and chapels, has been worked since medieval times. Its depth (500 ft/150 metres) is so great that from the viewing area men are the size of pinheads. Uses for the beautiful blue-grey slate are explored in the showroom.

A short distance north along the B3314 is the **Delabole Wind Farm**, which has 10 (surprisingly quiet) giant turbines. The Gaia Energy Centre next door closed at the end of 2004.

CAMELFORD

At a junction with the A39 turn right for **Camelford**. The long downhill street to the bridge over the River Camel has some attractive buildings. At the entrance to the town is the ★ **North Cornwall Museum and Gallery** (open Apr–Sept: Mon–Sat 10am–5pm). Country trades – those of farmer, cider-maker, carpenter, saddler, cooper, blacksmith – are well represented in re-creating life in moorland parishes more than a century ago. It is privately-owned and recently won a 'best small museum in Britain award'. A helpful tourist office is located in the same building.

The first right-hand turning from the hill above the Camel bridge allows the closest approach by car to ★ **Rough Tor** (1,312 ft/400 metres), which is one of Bodmin Moor's two principal heights (the other is Brown Willy). From the car park, well-beaten paths cross the granite-strewn slopes to the summit, which Bronze Age hut circles share with a memorial to the Wessex Regiment.

Returning to Camelford, a narrow lane on the other side of the A39 crosses a stream at **Slaughterbridge**, the site of King Arthur's last battle and his death. The **Arthurian Centre** (open daily 10am–dusk) has a 'Land of Arthur' exhibition, and a Grail Trail. By the crossroads, at the old station of a long-closed railway, is the **British Cycling Museum** (open Sun–Thur 10am–5pm) with more than 400 bikes and a history of cycling since 1818.

Map on page 70

TINTAGEL

★ **Tintagel**, suffused with Arthurian legend, is hugely popular. The castle alone receives over 130,000 visitors a year, so don't look for mystical tranquillity. Go late in the afternoon, if you can, when the coach parties will have departed. As you enter the village, **King Arthur's Great Halls** (open daily 10am–5pm) are straight in front of you, in Fore Street, offering a crash course in the Arthurian Experience – Arthur's story in laser lights, music and sound.

The ★ **Old Post Office** (NT; open mid-Mar–Jul and Sept–Oct: Sun–Fri 11am–5.30pm; Aug: daily 11am–5.30pm) is a short way down the road. This 14th-century manor house, which was for 50 years a post office, is furnished and managed by the National Trust, its letter-receiving function restored.

★★ **Tintagel Castle** (EH; open Easter–Sept: daily 10am–6pm; Oct: 10am–5pm; Nov–Mar: 10am–4pm) is a short walk from the village. It is amazing that so much of it survives, ravaged as it has been by time, the elements and neglect. The site, a headland that is almost an island, accessible only by a footbridge, is set in a coastline of dramatic black and craggy cliffs, exposed to the fury of the Atlantic. Celts followed Romans to the island, but their monastery and presence had disappeared by the time the Normans began building another chapel and a Great Hall. Henry

Star Attraction
● **Tintagel Castle**

Below: Tintagel Castle is set on a dramatic headland
Bottom: the Old Post Office

III's brother Richard, Earl of Cornwall, began a castle in the 13th century, which 300 years later had become 'sore wetherbeten and yn ruin'.

SHRINE AND VALLEY

North of Tintagel, beyond Bossiney, the B3263 crosses a stream opposite a parking place for ★ **Rocky Valley**. A path from the rocky Valley Centre leads to ★ **St Nectan's Glen**, with a 60-ft (18-metre) waterfall and a shrine called St Nectan's Kieve (open daily 10.30am–6.30pm or dusk). Many people regard the shrine as a sacred site, and the waterfall has been designated a Site of Special Scientific Interest (SSSI).

Below: Boscastle's harbour
Bottom: one of Boscastle's ancient whitewashed cottages

You reach ★★ **Boscastle** by way of Paradise, the hilltop area around the Napoleon Inn, and descend, on the right, the steep village street lined with ancient, whitewashed cottages. From the main car park a path follows the beautiful Valency Valley to the church of ★ **St Juliot**, where the young Thomas Hardy met his first wife, Emma, sister-in-law of the rector. In August 2004 a flash flood, created by a fierce rain storm, rushed down the valley in a matter of minutes. Despite devastation to property, there was no loss of life, and the people of Boscastle have worked flat out to restore their village. The fascinating **Museum of Witchcraft** manged to recover most of its

exhibits, and re-opened at Easter 2005. The Boscastle Tourist Office (tel: 01840-250010) and the Tintagel office (tel: 01840-779084) have a helpful website, www.visitboscastleandtintagel.com with details on accommodation and activities.

Star Attractions
● Boscastle
● Morwenstow

BUDE

From Boscastle, the B3263 joins the A39 for ★ **Bude**. The river struggles through the sand to the Haven, dividing the bathers and surfers of Summerleaze and Crooklets beaches, and the golfers and tennis players on the cliffs above, from the castle in the dunes and the canal on the south side. **Bude Canal**, begun in 1823 with the intention of linking the Bristol and English channels, reached no further than Launceston, and the arrival of the railway in the 1890s ended its working life. Only a short length of water remains.

Its history is told in the ★ **Bude–Stratton Museum** (open Easter–Oct: daily noon–5pm) on Lower Wharf. In the landscaped area behind it, Bude's flag flies over the council's offices in the tiny fort; this was built as a seaside residence in 1850 by Sir Goldsworthy Gurney, inventor of one of the earliest steam locomotives, and of the Bude Light, which was used to illuminate the House of Commons. In front of the fort is a slender, coloured concrete cone, a Millennium Project called the Bude Light 2000.

> **Hawker's legacy**
> For over 40 years, from 1834 to 1875, the Rev. Robert Hawker was parson of St John's church in Morwenstow. An eccentric but compassionate man, he gave Christian burial to sailors from ships wrecked below the treacherous cliffs. In the churchyard is the figurehead of the *Caledonia*, the sailing ship from Arbroath in Scotland whose crew found a resting place here in 1842.
>
> Hawker also revived a pagan custom when he gave an autumn thanksgiving service in his church in 1843: Harvest Festival, as it became known, is now so much a part of church ritual that it is easy to forget that it was virtually Hawker's creation.

THE VICAR OF MORWENSTOW

The A39 continues towards the Devon village of Welcombe. Two diversions can be made en route: first to the beautiful **Coombe Valley**; second to ★★ **Morwenstow**, Cornwall's northernmost point. This was the parish of the eccentric 19th-century vicar, Robert Hawker *(see box)*. Near the top of the treacherous cliffs is **Hawker's Hut**, the timber-framed shack where he watched out for ships in danger, mourned his wife and sought inspiration for his poetry. It is under the protection of the National Trust and must be its smallest property.

Beach huts at Bude

Painting and Sculpture

The special quality of Cornish scenery, the luminosity of the light and its heightening effect on colour have attracted many artists, but few have been natives. Among those who were, Cornish-born John Opie and Henry Bone both found fame in London. Bone, son of a Truro cabinet-maker, became a Royal Academician and official enamel painter to royalty. Opie, born in Harmony Cot near St Agnes in 1761, became a fashionable portrait painter, compared favourably by Sir Joshua Reynolds to Caravaggio. He was made a Royal Academician in 1787, but his talent declined into what his critics called 'tasteless face-painting'.

Sculpture in 19th-century Cornwall begins and ends with one man, Nevill Northy Burnard, born in 1818 at Altarnun on the eastern fringe of Bodmin Moor. The village has two significant examples of his carving: a slate tomb to the Isbells in the church, and a bust of John Wesley in a niche on the Wesleyan Chapel. Truro has his full-length figure of the explorer Richard Lander on the lofty monument at the top of Lemon Street.

THE NEWLYN SCHOOL

Cornwall's golden age of painting dawned in the 1880s in the fishing village of Newlyn, and later spread to St Ives. Inspired by the French *en plein air* style, the artists worked out of doors, painting the rocky landscapes, picturesque cottages and fishing boats, as well as the fishing community.

The Newlyn School centred around Samuel John 'Lamorna' Birch, Norman Garstin, Stanhope and Elizabeth Forbes, and Frank Bramley. Garstin's evocative work, *The Rain it Raineth Every Day* is in Penzance's Penlee House Gallery, as is Bramley's powerful *Hopeless Dawn* and many other fine works of the period.

In the early years of the 20th century, Lowell Dyer, with the support of Julius Olsson, set up the St Ives Arts Club – which also had literary members, like Havelock Ellis and Sir Leslie Stephen, father of Virginia Woolf and Vanessa Bell.

Opposite: Barbara Hepworth's sculpture garden
Below: Bernard Leach at work in his studio

ST IVES SOCIETY OF ARTISTS

In the 1920s, the St Ives Society of Artists was founded, its leading members being seascape painter Borlase Smart and John Park, a student of Olsson's. In the 1930s, painting in Cornwall was exposed to winds of change from the continent. Ben Nicholson's work was beginning to be influenced by his friendship with Mondrian and Braque. With his wife, Winifred, he made his home in St Ives. The potter Bernard Leach was already working there, in a studio that still stands.

Below: Alfred Wallis: Steamship in Harbour
Bottom: John Park: The Morning Ride

Over the next decade, other artists gathered, among them John Wells, David Haughton, Wilhelmina Barns-Graham and Peter Lanyon, the only locally-born artist among them.

In the 1930s Nicholson and Christopher Wood met the fisherman and scrap merchant, Alfred Wallis, whose untutored oil paintings on scraps of card showing ships, harbours and lighthouses were inspirational.

Shortly before World War II sculptor Barbara Hepworth came to St Ives (she later married Nicholson). She set up Trewyn Studio and worked there until her death in a fire in 1975. The studio is now a gallery, under the auspices of Tate St Ives, which celebrated the centenary of her birth in 2003. Numerous galleries in St Ives and elsewhere, showing the work of contemporary artists, prove that art in Cornwall is alive and well.

Architecture and Design

The Normans were the first group to have an architectural influence on Cornwall, thrusting defensive buildings on their newly acquired territory. At Launceston and Tremanton, near Saltash, castle keeps and walls commanded the main routes into the county, and at Restormel is the finest Norman keep of all.

CHURCH ARCHITECTURE

It is to church architecture, though, that the Normans brought special concern. At St Germans, near Saltash, once the seat of the bishop, the twin-towered west front of the cathedral-sized church has a wonderful carved stone portal. The style of Cornwall's medieval churches is dictated by the local stone, and the treatment of interiors is diverse. Bench-ends, especially, offered their designers unlimited opportunities for imagination and self-expression, as in the superb examples at Altarnun. Minor architectural glories shelter holy wells like St Cleer, a simple, unfussy statement in granite.

It makes a nice contrast to two of Cornwall's most flamboyant ecclesiastical gestures: the intricately carved and decorated granite exterior of 16th-century St Mary Magdalene in Launceston; and elegant Truro Cathedral, J. L. Pearson's amazingly successful exercise in 19th-century French Gothic.

COUNTRY HOUSES

The county is rich in great country houses. Cotehele, high above the banks of the Tamar, with a richly decorated arch-braced roof to the Great Hall, is little altered since the 15th century. Elizabethan Trerice near Newquay, home of the Arundells, although on a modest scale, has a front with three Dutch-style gables, behind which the hall rises through two storeys, with good plasterwork ceilings both here and in the drawing room.

The Elizabethan front is echoed in Lanherne, near St Columb, the house the Arundells gave

Georgian buildings
Some of the best Georgian architecture in Cornwall is to be found in the broad sweep of Lemon Street in Truro. Elsewhere, Liskeard has some elegant 18th-century buildings, and there are a few notable examples in Castle Street, Launceston, especially Lawrence House, now a small museum.

Stained glass in St Germans

*Below: the Classic severity
of Pencarrow
Bottom: Daphne du Maurier*

to nuns displaced by the French Revolution. Prideaux Place in Padstow is in the more traditional early 17th-century 'E' shape, with a long castellated façade and an extension in Georgian Gothic. Splendid Lanhydrock, near Lostwithiel, has a superb setting in a landscaped park, and is arranged around a courtyard. Only one wing survives of the 17th-century house, which was burnt in 1881, but it has been rebuilt along the original lines. An outstanding feature is the 1658 gatehouse, sprouting exuberant obelisks.

At Torpoint, just a ferry ride away from Plymouth, is the elegant Antony House, a Palladian exercise by an unknown architect, set within embracing brick walls, that is the most distinguished of its time in the county. Later houses present a tug-of-war between styles, swinging between John Nash's romantic Gothic Caerhays Castle and the Classic severity of both Trelissik and Pencarrow.

Literary Cornwall

Many writers have come to Cornwall seeking isolation. Others have fallen in love with the place and been drawn back over the years.

D. H. Lawrence's association was short yet productive. Seeking distance from London and World War I, he set up a small community in Zennor, but internal dissent and a brush with the military, when the Lawrences were suspected of spying, forced them to leave. However, much of *Women in Love* and 'The Nightmare' chapter in *Kangaroo* were written here.

Daphne du Maurier's novels spring from her passionate interest in the romantic associations of Cornish places and people. Jamaica Inn on Bodmin Moor owes its fascination as much to her writing as to any association with smuggling. Her early novels were written at Bodinnick near Fowey, and *The King's General* during her long residence at Menabilly, the Rashleighs' house.

Thomas Hardy came to Cornwall in 1870 as a young architect to restore the church of St Juliot in Valency Valley near Boscastle. He married

the rector's sister-in-law, Emma, in London, and only returned to Cornwall after her early death.

A. L. Rowse, the great authority on Elizabethan England, wrote *A Cornish Childhood* about his upbringing among the spoil-heaps of St Austell's china clay fringes. Sir Arthur Quiller-Couch was born in Bodmin in 1863 but identified with Fowey, the 'Troy Town' in his stories. For 50 years 'Q', as he was known, lived at The Haven, where the ferry crosses to Polruan. Kenneth Grahame was a frequent visitor. Grahame began *The Wind in the Willows* while in Falmouth.

Virginia Woolf spent childhood holidays in St Ives, and her memories of Godrevy Lighthouse across the bay contributed to her novel *To the Lighthouse* and to *Jacob's Room* and *The Waves*.

Robert Stephen Hawker was born in Plymouth in 1803 and came to Morwenstow, on the wild north coast, as minister in 1834, and stayed for 40 years. As well as his parish duties he wrote commendable poetry, and composed *The Song of the Western Men (Trelawny)*, which the Cornish adopted as their national anthem *(see page 83)*.

Winston Graham, in his immensely popular *Poldark* novels, draws on the 19th-century mining industry around Perranporth and St Agnes.

Sir John Betjeman's childhood holidays were spent in Trebetherick, just above Daymer Bay at the mouth of the Camel estuary *(see box)*.

> **Poet's inspiration**
> Poet Laureate John Betjeman (1906–84) developed a deep love for North Cornwall, which inspired some of his early poems, propelling him by bicycle on visits to churches, as he wrote in his verse autobiography *Summoned by Bells*. He really enjoyed the ferry journey to Padstow, or arriving there by 'the best train journey I know', from Wadebridge.
>
> Fittingly, the old station building in Wadebridge is now the John Betjeman Centre *(see page 70).*

Virginia Woolf with her father, Sir Leslie Stephen

Festivals

Bodmin Ridings: first Sat in July. Pageant commemorates a rebellion in 1549 against the introduction of the *Book of Common Prayer* in English.

Camborne, Trevethick Day: last Sat in April. Richard Trevethick, who designed the first railway locomotive and a high-pressure steam pumping engine for the tin mines, is remembered in the Trevethick Dance, a parade of steam engines.

Dehwelans Festival: May Day weekend. Based in Newquay this new festival (initiated in 2003) celebrates all things Cornish.

Golowan Festival and Mazey Day: early June. Penzance's two-week festival culminates with Mazey Day, and the Feast of St John, with music, theatre, craft fairs and processions.

Helston Flora Day: 8 May. Processions and rowdy celebrations of spring, including a processional, jigging dance called the Furry Dance.

Padstow May Day: 1 May. The 'Obby Oss', a horse-like creature in black mask and hooped skirt, is carried through the streets, followed by dancers.

Royal Cornwall Show, near Wadebridge: second week in June. A three-day agricultural show, that is also a celebration of work and leisure.

St Columb Major Hurling Match: Shrove Tuesday. Competing teams grapple for possession of a silver-coated apple-wood ball.

Shark Angling Festival

An interesting, albeit less traditional, event takes place in Looe in late June – the Shark Angling Festival. The Shark Angling Club was formed in 1953, and during the sport's heyday in the late 1950s and early 1960s between 5,000 and 6,000 sharks were caught annually. Numbers have since declined dramatically. The club operates a 'tag and release' policy to ensure that numbers are preserved, and insists that none of the sharks are landed. To find out more, tel: 01503-262642.

Sheep shearing demonstration at the Royal Cornwall Show

St Ives September Fringe Festival. One of the top arts and music festivals in the West Country. Classical music, jazz, folk, comedy and poetry; numerous art events, workshops and exhibitions, with an international line up of performers.

Music and Theatre

Cornwall's traditional music has a strong Celtic element, although musicologists believe it has more in common with the folk music of Brittany than with that of Wales or Ireland. The Cornish tradition came close to dying out, but is enjoying a revival, with young bands and singers performing live and making recordings. Bands feature instruments such as the Cornish bagpipes, the *krowd* (a three-stringed fiddle), organ, flute and harp. Lyrics, of course, are sung in Cornish. Cornwall also has a number of theatres *(see below)* and the Cornish-based Knee High Theatre Company is receiving national aclaim.

Sir Malcolm Arnold, who wrote the Four Cornish Dances

CORNISH PRIDE

The best known pieces of music associated with Cornwall are *Trelawny*, the 'Cornish national anthem', written by the Rev. Hawker *(see page 75)* in 1825, celebrating the acquittal of Bishop Jonathan Trelawny in a 17th-century libel case; and Malcolm Arnold's *Four Cornish Dances* and *Padstow Lifeboat March*, the latter written in 1967 as a tribute to the Padstow lifeboat crews.

VENUES

The splendid Hall for Cornwall in Truro hosts a varied programme of music, from pop to classical and ballet (tel: 01872-262466), plus drama. For classical music in a traditional setting, attend the St Endellion Music Festivals in spring and summer (tel: 01208-850463). The Acorn Theatre, Penzance (tel: 01736-365520) offers a year-round professional programme of theatre, comedy and music; while Minack Theatre *(see page 53)* stages dramatic performances in a stunning setting.

FOOD AND DRINK

Cornwall has many traditional foods, but the Cornish pasty has become symbol as much as sustenance. Essentially an early form of 'fast food' with real rib-sticking nourishment, the pasty evolved as an all-in-one lunch for miners, fishermen and farmers. A real Cornish pasty is a crescent-shaped pie of shortcrust pastry, crimped along one side. The traditional filling is chuck steak, chopped turnip, potatoes and onion, liberally seasoned with salt and pepper. Once upon a time, one end would include the above mixture, while the other was filled with jam or treacle, providing a two-course meal. How the two fillings were prevented from leaking into each other has never been satisfactorily explained.

PIES

It's a short step from pasties to pies, and here the Cornish cook is resourceful. Squab pie is filled, not with young pigeons as the name suggests, but with a delicious mixture of lamb, apple, onions and sometimes prunes; and giblet pie is made from the neck and liver of a goose. But the favourite is Stargazy pie, once made with pilchards and now with mackerel; the fish, cleaned and boned, are laid on a pastry base with their heads poking out through a pastry lid, and the gaps between them filled with chopped bacon and hard-boiled egg.

SEAFOOD

The most traditional Cornish food is found in the seafood restaurants. You can expect salmon from the Tamar and the Camel on menus in those areas, and farmed trout almost everywhere.

Driftwood Spars Hotel,
St Agnes

Mackerel is a ubiquitous fish, delicious baked in vinegar, flavoured with onion and bay leaves. But best in the west of the county are lobster and crab, served in a variety of ways; and oysters from Helford River. Newlyn crab chowder should not be missed.

DESSERTS AND CHEESE

Desserts weigh in heavily; figgy pudding is baked with suet, flour, eggs, sugar and raisins (not figs). Heavy cake speaks for itself. Lighter alternatives are saffron buns and saffron cake; even lighter are Cornish splits, cut in half and buttered and at their wicked best with clotted cream and jam. Substitute treacle for jam and you have 'thunder and lightning'.

Treacle, or golden syrup, is also used in Cornish fairings, biscuits with a crackled top and flavouring of ground ginger and cinnamon.

Cornish yarg cheese, wrapped in nettles, has recently been making a name for itself. It is produced by Lynher Farms & Dairies Upton Cross, near Liskeard, tel: 01579-362244.

Mead and ale

Metheglin (Cornish mead) is available in many local inns. Made from fermented honey, it is produced at several meaderies in the far west, notably Callestock near Perranporth, where cider and preserves can also be obtained, and at Penzance and St Agnes.

The choice of beers is rather limited to the spheres of influence of St Austell Brewery and the Cornish Brewery at Redruth, but there is the long-established Blue Anchor Inn at Helston, where 'Spingo', of varying strengths, reigns supreme, and some enterprising newcomers such as Sharp's at Pityme near Rock in North Cornwall.

Restaurants

Cornwall once offered fairly basic menus, but nowadays chefs are developing exciting new dishes that take advantage of the county's superb fresh produce from land and, especially, sea. Inns also offer meals that go far beyond basic pub food.

Prices are based on a three-course meal for two with house wine: £££ = over £70, ££ = £50–70, £ = under £50.

Bude
Villa Restaurant, 16 The Strand, tel: 01288-354799. The fish, meat and fresh vegetables are excellent and the wine list extensive, so try to ignore the vivid decor. ££–£££

Falmouth
Harbourside Restaurant, Harbourside, tel: 01326-312440. In the Greenbank Hotel, with stunning views. Specialises in fish, but meat dishes are also interesting. Selection of West Country cheeses. ££–£££

Fowey
Food For Thought, 4 Town Quay, tel: 0871 426 4550. First-class fish and seafood dishes, and equally good meat; in the centre of the village. ££
Q Restaurant, 28 Fore Street, tel: 01726-833302. Part of the Old Quay House Hotel, right on the estuary. Fish, of course, but meat too. Daily specials and an interesting wine list. ££

Launceston
Ye Olde Bell Inn, 1 Tower Street, tel: 01566-775154. The oldest pub in town serves traditional home-cooked dishes and spares a thought for vegetarians. Restaurant open 10am–9pm. £–££

Mousehole
Old Coastguard Inn, The Parade, tel: 01736-731222. This old inn on the outskirts of the village featured in the *Good Pub Guide 2003*. Seafood and sea views are the specialities. ££–£££

Mylor
Pandora Inn, Restronguet Creek, tel: 01326-372678. Great waterside atmosphere in a slate-floored thatched inn, where the emphasis is on Cornish produce, especially seafood. ££

Padstow
The Seafood Restaurant, Riverside, tel: 01841-532700. Celebrity chef's celebrated restaurant. Advance booking essential. Superb fish dishes. £££
Rick Stein's Café, 8 Middle Street, tel: 01841-532700. A less expensive version of the above, in a pleasant wood-panelled restaurant. Booking advisable for dinner. ££
St Petroc's Bistro, 4 New Street, tel: 01841-532700. More of the same in Stein's own small hotel. He also has a fish and chip shop (eat in or take away) on South Quay (£). £££
No 6, Art & Seafood Café, 6 Middle Street, tel: 01841-532093. Stein's impact has raised the culinary tone of the whole town. This pleasant restaurant does a very good set price menu. ££–£££

Tea rooms

It's hard to think of a town or village in Cornwall that does not have at least one tea room. In the more popular spots, they vie for trade. Many of them have tables set out in attractive gardens, others have scenic settings, overlooking a beach or harbour. Some have a habit of closing at 5pm, which most people consider is still tea time. Most of them serve a slap-up tea of scones, or Cornish splits, with lashings of cream, jam and butter. And if you fancy a change, saffron cake is usually on offer as well. For details on recommended tea rooms, visit www.teacouncil.co.uk

Penzance

Abbey Restaurant, Abbey Street, tel: 01736-330680. Reliably good and imaginative dishes served, very pleasantly, in an attractive first-floor dining room with sea views. **££–£££**
Summer House Restaurant, Cornwall Terrace, tel: 01736-363744. Excellent Mediterranean cuisine in a stylish Regency building with a garden, near the promenade. **££–£££**

Porthleven, nr Helston

Critchards Seafood Restaurant, The Harbour Head, tel: 01326-562407. Featured in the *Good Food Guide*. Imaginative fish dishes in pleasant surroundings. Evenings only. Booking advisable. **£££**

Newquay

Beach Hut Bistro, Watergate Bay, tel: 01637-860840. Cheerful and extremely popular, with stunning sea views, good fish dishes and sundowner cocktails. Best to book. **£–££**
Fifteen Cornwall, Watergate Bay, tel: 01637-861000. Jamie Oliver's Cornish venture. Excellent fresh fish, and organic produce from the nearby Buttervilla Farm Hotel. **£££**
Finn's Restaurant, Old Fishing Harbour (off South Quay Hill), tel: 01637-874062. Fish and seafood in some interesting combinations; specialises in lobster; lunchtime dishes are less expensive. **££–£££**

St Ives

Alba, Old Lifeboat House, Wharf Road, tel: 0871 811 4457. Cool, minimalist place with uninterrupted harbour views from the first-floor dining toom. Cod wrapped in pancetta and squid with blood pudding are among the well-prepared options. **££–£££**
Porthminster Beach Café, Porthminster Beach, tel: 01736-795352. Excellent, mainly fish, dishes, delicious puddings, unsurpassed views. Morning coffee, afternoon tea. **££**

St Mawes

Water's Edge, Idle Rocks Hotel, Harbourside, tel: 0132-270771/0844 502 7587. British and French dishes, using local ingredients when possible; great views. Book at weekends and in high season. **£££**

Truro

Sevens, 77 Lemon Street, tel: 01872 275767. Modern European food in pleasant surroundings in the heart of town. Not cheap, but worth it. **£££**

Country pubs are welcoming and the standard of food is usually high

ACTIVE HOLIDAYS

SURFING

Cornwall's exhilarating Atlantic coast offers some of the best surfing in the country. When the waves are right, surfers converge on the beaches and sometimes don't leave until the light fades. Surfing is at its best at Fistral Bay, Lusty Glaze and Watergate Bay, Newquay, and Porthmeor Beach, St Ives, but Bude, St Agnes and Perranporth are also strong contenders.

In all these places you can hire and, of course, buy equipment, take lessons, and be assured of qualified instructors and lifeguards. All the schools listed below have the British Surfing Association seal of approval. In Newquay, the Dolphin Surf School (17 Eliot Gardens, tel: 01637-873707 or 07974-629381; www.surf-school.co.uk) offers tuition by the day or week, with all-in-prices for lessons, equipment, wetsuits, and accommodation if required . Also in Newquay, the Reef Surf School (27 Agar Road, tel: 01637-879058; www.reefsurfschool.com) offers similar deals. Many shops in the town hire or sell equipment.

In St Ives, the Porthmeor Beach Café and Surf Centre (tel: 01736-793366), offers tuition and equipment hire; as does the St Ives Surf School (tel: 0966-498021), also on Porthmeor Beach. The Natural Balance Surf Co (14 Fore Street, tel: 01736-793264), hires and sells gear and has a good café upstairs, The Storm in a Teacup. In nearby Hayle, try the Shore Surf School (46 Mount Pleasant, St. Ives Bay, tel: 01736-755556).

In Widemouth Bay, Bude, the environmentally-aware Outdoor Adventure Multi-Activity and Surf School (tel: 01288-362900, www.outdooradventure.co.uk) specialises in yachting and canoeing as well as surfing, and offers accommodation. In Perranporth, the Blue Wings Surf School (tel: 01637-874445), gives lessons.

For up-to-the-minute tide and wind conditions and the best surfing spots, check www.bbc.co.uk/cornwall/surfing or contact Surfcall, tel: 09068-360360. In West Penwith (for St Ives and Sennen Cove) information can also be gained on tel: 01891-333080.

CYCLING

For cycling to or around the Eden Project, contact Bugle Cycle Hire: tel: 01237-424123; www.buglecyclehire.co.uk. For the Camel Trail, Bridge Bike Hire, tel: 01208-813050 (see page 71); or Padstow Cycle Hire, tel: 01841-533533. For coast-to-coast tramways (Portreath to Devoran), try Bissoe Tramways Cycle Hire, tel: 01872-870341. For general information, check www.nationalcyclenetwork.org.uk

SAILING

The Fal and Camel estuaries offer some fine sailing. Details from sailing clubs at Falmouth, tel: 01326-211223; Fowey, tel: 01726-832335; Flushing, tel: 01326-374043; Helford River, tel:

🦅 Bird watching

The Fal Estuary, Gerrans Bay and the surrounding coastline are ideal spots for keen birdwatchers. A huge number of seabirds, divers, waders and sea ducks are either resident here or regular winter visitors. Most of this coastline is managed by the National Trust and there are footpaths along much of its length. For more details, contact Mike Lord at the Cornwall Bird-watching and Preservation Society, Gue Gossel, The Lizard, TR12 7PH; or Andrea Toy at the Cornwall Wildlife Trust, Five Acres, Allet, Truro TR4 9DJ.

01326-231460; Looe, tel: 01503-262559; or tel: 01872-864295; Mylor, tel: 01326-374391; Rock, tel: 01208-862431; St Mawes, tel: 01326-270686; St Mary's, Isles of Scilly, tel: 01720-422208. South West Lakes Trust also runs watersports centres; tel: 01837-871565, www.swlakestrust.org.uk

FISHING

Information about fishing can be obtained from South West Water Leisure Services, Higher Coombepark, Lewdon, Okehampton, Devon EX20 4QT, tel: 01837-871565.

RIDING AND PONY TREKKING

Licensed establishments offering riding and trekking for all ages and abilities include: Denby Riding Stables, Nanstallon, nr Bodmin, tel: 01208-72013; Efford Down Riding Stables, Bude, tel: 01288-354 244; Penhalwyn Trekking Centre and School, Goon Mine Mellyn, Halsetown, St Ives, tel: 01736-796461; Tresallyn Riding Stables, Padstow, tel: 01840-520454.

GOLF

Cornish links are often set in superb coastal sites. Try the Bude and North Cornwall Golf Club, Burn View, tel: 01288-352006. Mullion Golf Club, tel: 01326-240685, is on a cliff top.

St Enedoc Golf Club, Rock, tel: 01208-83216, has two courses, as does St Mellion Golf Club, Saltash, tel: 01579-351351, where one is designed by Jack Nicklaus. For more details, visit: www.golfincornwall.co.uk

FLYING

Contact the Cornish Gliding and Flying Club, Perranporth Airfield, tel: 01872-572124, Cornwall Flying Club, Bodmin Airfield, Cardinham, tel: 01208-821419; or Moorland Flying Club, Camelford, tel: 01822-832.

WALKING

The South West Coastal Path, the Camel Trail and Cardinham Woods all offer great walking. For information on the South West Path, tel: 01752-896237; www.swcp.org.uk The Coast & Countryside Service offers guided walks in North Cornwall, tel: 01840-250010. Cornwall's Mineral Tramways, have been restored and opened as walking and cycling tracks, tel: 01872-222000 for details *(see pages 61 and 63)*. For information on the 2004 'Right to Roam' legislation, check www.countrysideaccess.gov.uk, or call tel: 08451-003298.

Cornwall's Atlantic coast offers the best surfing in the country

PRACTICAL INFORMATION

Getting There

BY TRAIN

InterCity trains, operated by First Great Western, run from London Paddington to various towns in Cornwall. Most are direct but sometimes a change to a local train is necessary at Exeter or Plymouth. Direct journey time London–Truro about 5 hours; to Penzance about 6 hours.

Virgin Trains run from Birmingham, Bristol and cities in northern England and Scotland; www.virgintrains.co.uk. Wales and West Passenger Trains have services from Birmingham, Bath, Swindon and Cardiff.

For all train information, contact National Rail Enquiries, tel: 08457-484950; www.nationalrail.com Tickets can also be purchased on-line, and there are various deals, subject to availability, if booked more than a week in advance, but they sell out fairly fast.

BY ROAD

The nearest motorway to Cornwall, the M5 (connections with the M4 at Bristol and the M5 at Birmingham) ends at Exeter, from where the main routes into Cornwall are the A30 to Penzance and the A38 to Bodmin via Plymouth, both of which have large sections of dual carriageway. North Cornwall is served by the Atlantic Highway (A39).

BY COACH

National Express runs services from London, Heathrow Airport, and most parts of the country to Truro and Penzance, plus a number of other towns. Journey time London–Truro is about 6½ hours; to Penzance about 8½ hours. Tickets bought in advance are cheaper. For further information: www.nationalexpress.com or tel: 0870-580 8080.

BY AIR

There are airports at Plymouth and Newquay. Air Southwest flies to both from London Gatwick four times a day, daily from Manchester, Bristol and Leeds Bradford. For information and bookings: tel: 0870-241 8202; www.airsouthwest.com. Ryanair flies from London Stansted to Newquay once a day, tel: 0871-246 0000; www.ryanair.co.uk British Airways has a daily flight from Gatwick to Newquay, www.ba.com (flight time from London about 1¼ hours). For all Newquay Airport enquiries, tel: 01637-860600, or www.newquaynet.com/newquay_airport.htm. For Plymouth, tel: 01752-204090 or www.plymouthcity.co.uk/airport.htm.

To the Isles of Scilly

British International operates helicopter services between Penzance and Tresco and St Mary's, tel: 01736-363871; for bookings on day of departure, tel: 01736-364296. The Isles of Scilly Steamship Group's Skybus (fixed wing) operates flights Mon–Sat to St Mary's from Land's End, Newquay, Exeter and Bristol (connecting with Air Southwest flights). This company's *Scillonian III* sails from Penzance to St Mary's, sailing time approximately 2 hours 40 minutes. Enquiries for Skybus and *Scillonian III*, tel: 08457-105555; www.newquaynet.com/newquay_airport.htm; advance bookings are essential.

Car hire

Check www.parkandsave.co.uk/car-hire/newquay-airport for major hire companies at Newquay Airport. Avis, Hertz and Europcar also have outlets in Truro, and the latter in Falmouth. Elsewhere, try local companies.

Getting Around

BY CAR

To steer clear of local traffic congestion, tune into BBC Radio Cornwall *(see page 92)* for regular bulletins on traffic hold-ups. Parking is often a problem in summer. Park & Ride rail schemes are run in high season at Liskeard (for Looe) and Lelant Saltings (for St Ives).

BY TRAIN

Regional Railways operate between Plymouth and Penzance via Liskeard and Truro, with lines heading off to Gunnislake, Looe, Newquay, Falmouth and St Ives. Three-day (any three days in a seven-day period) and eight-day (eight-days in a 15-day period) Cornish Rail Rover tickets offer considerable savings; for details visit www.carfreedaysout.com.

BY BUS

Local bus services are fairly reliable. For general information on bus and coach travel around Cornwall, ring the Traveline, tel: 0870-241 2216, or www.travelinesw.com. Other details are available from First Devon and Cornwall (previously Western National Bus Services, tel: 0870 608 2 608 or www.firstgroup.com/ukbus. Other services are run by Western Greyhound, tel: 01637-871871; www.westerngreyhound.com, which offers a Day Rover ticket; and Truronian, tel: 01872-273453; www.truronian.co.uk.

Around the Isles of Scilly

Inter-island boat services are run by St Mary's Boatmen's Association which has a ticket kiosk on the quay. On the other islands there are passenger services as well as bird-watching and sea-life spotting trips. Contact Bryher Boat Services, tel: 01720-422886, St Agnes Boating, tel: 01720-422704, www.st-agnes-boating.co.uk.

Facts for the Visitor

TOURIST INFORMATION

Cornwall looks after its visitors and there are signposted Tourist Information Centres in all the main towns and resorts. The central information service is VisitCornwall, Pydar House, Pydar Street, Truro, Cornwall TR1 1EA, tel: 01872-322900; www.cornwall-touristboard.co.uk. It can be contacted for advance information but it is not a drop-in tourist information centre.

Local tourist information offices usually keep normal office hours, although some have extended opening times in high season. They include: Bodmin, Shire House, Mount Folly Square, tel: 01208-76616; Boscastle Visitor Centre, Cobweb car park, tel: 01840-250010; Bude, Crescent car park, tel: 01288-354240; Falmouth, 11 Market Strand, Prince of Wales Pier, tel: 01326-312300; Fowey, 5 South Street, tel: 01726-833616; Helston and Lizard Peninsula, Isaac House, Tyacke Road, tel: 01209-614000; Isles of Scilly, Hugh Street, Hugh Town, St Mary's, tel: 01720-424031; Launceston, Market House Arcade, Market Street, tel: 01566-772333; Looe, The Guildhall, Fore Street, tel: 01503-262072; Megavissey, St George's Square, tel: 01726-844857; Newquay, Municipal Buildings, Marcus Hill, tel: 01637-854020; Padstow, Red Brick Building, North Quay, tel: 01841-533449; Penzance, Station Road, tel: 01736-362207; St Ives, Guildhall, Street an Pol, tel: 01736-796297; Tintagel, Bossiney Road, tel: 01840-779084; Truro, Municipal Offices, Boscawen Street, tel: 01872-274555.

Some useful websites include: www.swtourism.co.uk, www.cornwall-calling.co.uk, www.cornwall-online.co.uk, www.chycor.co.uk, www.connexions.co.uk, www.cornish-riviera.org.uk, www.cornishlight.com, www.isles-of-scilly.co.uk and www.wildlifetrust.org.uk

OPENING TIMES

Most shops open from 9am to 5.30pm; supermarkets usually stay open later, and some now open on Sunday. Post offices open Monday–Friday 9am to 5.30pm, and usually till noon on Saturday. Banks open Monday–Friday 9am–4.30pm. Some museums and attractions, and most gardens, are open only between Easter and October, and others have restricted opening times in winter. Opening times for major attractions are mentioned in the relevant sections of this guide. There are plenty of late-night garages.

LOCAL MEDIA

For local news and details of upcoming events, refer to the *Cornish Guardian* or the weekly *Cornishman*, or visit www.thisiscornwall.co.uk, BBC Radio Cornwall; FM: 103.9 MHz in mid and west Cornwall; 98.2 MHz in north and east Cornwall. Medium Wave: 650KHz in mid- and west Cornwall; 657 KHz in north and east Cornwall.

CLEAN BEACHES

Local tourist offices can advise on which beaches have consistently passed the EU Bathing Water Direc-

There is a variety of beaches, from sheltered coves to sandy stretches

tive. The cleanest beaches in Cornwall include Sandy Mouth, Bude; Harlyn Bay; Treyarnon Bay and neighbouring Constantine Bay, near Padstow; Porthmeor and Porthminster; St Ives; Whitesand Bay, near Land's End; Lusty Glaze Beach, Newquay; and Praa Sands, near Helston. In order to maintain standards of cleanliness, dogs are not allowed on many Cornish beaches between Easter and October. For detailed information on clean bathing in Cornwall, consult *The Good Beach Guide* (Reader's Digest).

MEDICAL ASSISTANCE

Nationals of the European Union are entitled to free medical treatment in any part of the UK. Some other countries also have reciprocal arrangements for free treatment. However, most visitors from abroad have to pay for medical and dental services and should ensure that they have adequate health insurance.

The Royal Cornwall Hospital in Truro has a full Accident and Emergency (A&E) Department, and the West Cornwall Hospital in Penzance has a 24-hour Casualty Department which deals with less serious cases.

For emergency ambulance, fire or police dial 999.

For Children

When it's too wet or too cold for the beach, here are some suggestions for places to take children:

Bodmin and Wenford Railway, Bodmin General Station, Bodmin, tel: 0845-1259678 (open Easter–Oct: daily, plus special events all year including Christmas Santa Specials). Assorted steam and diesel locomotives, plus two branch lines.

Dairyland Farm World, Summercourt, 4 miles (7 km) from Newquay, tel: 01872-510246 (open Easter–Oct: daily 10am–5pm). Giant milking parlour. Country life museum. Pets, ponies and nature trails.

Dobwalls Family Adventure Park, near Liskeard (open Apr–Sept: daily 10.30am–5pm; rest of year: tel: 01579-320325). Trips on extensive miniature railway with steam and diesel locomotives. Large adventure playground. Re-opens in 2008 after extensive renovation.

The Flambards Experience, Culdrose Manor, Helston, 24-hr infoline tel:0845 601 8684 (open Easter–Oct: daily 10.30am; late Jul–Aug: 10am; last admission 3.30pm). Large theme park with a funfair with log flume and roller coaster, as well as more adult attractions (*see page 46*).

The Monkey Sanctuary, B3253, Murrayton, Looe, tel: 01503-262532 (open Easter–Sept: Sun–Thurs 11am–4.30pm). Descendants of a colony of rescued woolly monkeys kept in an environment as similar as possible to their natural one.

National Maritime Museum, Falmouth, tel: 01326-313388 (open daily 10am–5pm). Lots to interest children of all ages at this popular attraction (*see page 41 for details*).

National Seal Sanctuary, Gweek, Helston, tel: 01326-221361 (open daily 10am–5pm). Resident seals and sea-lions. Nature trails, play areas. Feeding times are usually around 11am–noon and 2.30pm, but variable.

Paradise Park, Hayle, tel: 01736-751020 (open daily 10am; last entry summer 5pm; winter 3pm) Remarkable collection of rare birds, and penguins. Home of the World Parrot Trust and Cornish Otter Sanctuary. Eagle and falconry displays.

Screech Owl Sanctuary, nr Indian Queens, Goss Moor (off A30), tel: 01726-860182 (open Mar–Oct: daily 10am–6pm; Feb half-term: till 4pm). A fascinating education/conservation centre, with 36 owl species.

Shires Adventure Park, Trelow Farm, Tredinnick, Wadebridge, tel: 01841-541215 (open Easter–Sept: daily 10am–5pm; Oct: Sun–Fri). Shire horse shows; animals in Old Macdonald's Barn. Enchanted Forest, Haunted Castle, and the Dragon Kingdom, a huge indoor adventure zone.

World in Miniature, Goonhavern, nr Newquay, tel: 0870-458 4433 (open May–Oct: daily 10am–5pm). 12-acre (5-hectare) park with Jurassic Adventure World, crazy golf and a maze.

World of Model Railways, Mevagissey, tel: 01726-842457 (open Easter–Oct: daily 10am–5pm). 2,000 models; rail layout with 50 trains running through various landscapes.

Shopping for souvenirs

Apart from model lighthouses and whimsical piskies, the main things to buy in Cornwall, either as gifts or souvenirs, are food items – gift-wrapped boxes of fudge in numerous flavours are popular and so is clotted cream, if it isn't going to be taken on too long a journey.

Many visitors also like to buy paintings, drawings or ceramic pieces. There are plenty of galleries and shops to choose from, especially in St Ives, Marazion and Fowey, and some of the work is of very good quality. Most of the paintings are of local subjects, which makes them ideal mementoes of a holiday.

ACCOMMODATION

Cornwall offers just about every type of accommodation to suit your needs and pocket. Booking is essential during high summer, but not always at other times. VisitCornwall, Pydar House, Pydar Street, Truro, Cornwall TR1 1EA, tel: 01872-322900 will mail copies of their *Places to Stay Guide* . Their website: www.cornwalltouristboard.co.uk, also has a brochure line.

The following categories are for a double room with breakfast in midsummer: £££ = £150 or over; ££ = £80–£150; £ = under £80.

Bolventor
Jamaica Inn, nr Launceston, tel: 01566-86250; www.jamaicainn.co.uk The famous inn on the moor has recently expanded but retains its atmosphere – and its ghost. **££**

Carlyon
Carlyon Bay Hotel, Sea Road, tel: 01726-812304, fax: 01726-814938; www.brend-hotels.co.uk/carlyon Luxurious 1930s hotel set in 250 acres (100 hectares) of sub-tropical gardens, with leisure facilities, including golf. **£££**

Falmouth
Greenbank Hotel, Harbourside, tel: 01326-312440; www.greenbank-hotel.com Stunning harbour views; well-furnished rooms; smooth service. **££**
St Michael's, Stracey Road, tel: 01326-312707; fax: 01326-211772; www.corushotels.co.uk Great views over Gyllyngvase Beach from this sleek, refurbished hotel. Sub-tropical gardens; indoor pool and sauna. **£££**

Fowey
Old Quay House Hotel, 28 Fore Street, tel: 01726-833302; www.theoldquayhouse.com A new hotel in an old building, with 12 rooms, 7 with harbour views; minimalist decor. Pleasant service. No smoking. **££–£££**

Lamorna Cove
The Cove, tel: 01736-731411; www.thecovecornwall.com Comfortable, stylish and newly refurbished; lovely views of the cove. Good pool. **£££**

Mullion
Polurrian Hotel, tel: 01326-240421; www.polurrianhotel.com Set in 12-acre (5-hectare) gardens above a sandy cove; indoor and outdoor pools. **£££**

Newquay
Headland Hotel, tel: 01637-872211; www.headlandhotel.co.uk Imposing appearance but a family-friendly atmosphere. Set in 10 acres (4 hectares) above Fistral Beach, with a golf course. **£££**

Padstow
Tregea Hotel, 16–18 High Street, tel: 01871-871 2686; www.tregea.co.uk close to the harbour, a friendly, family-run hotel in a 17th-century building. **££**

Penzance
Abbey Hotel, Abbey Street, tel: 01736-366906, fax: 01736-351163. Delightful building overlooking harbour. Rooms are tastefully furnished. Cosy, excellent restaurant. **££–£££**
Tarbert Hotel, 11 Clarence Street, tel: 01736-363758; www.tarbert-hotel.co.uk A Georgian building with open fires. All rooms have sleek bathrooms. **££**

Polperro
Crumplehorn Mill Inn, tel: 01503-272348; www.crumplehorn-inn.co.uk Attractive complex of buildings centred on 14th-century mill. Cornish ales; good special breaks off-season. **£–££**

Talland Bay Hotel, tel: 01503-272667; www.tallandbayhotel.co.uk Between Polperro and Looe, overlooking Talland Bay. Comfortable; 2½-acre (1-hectare) garden, pool and quiet beach **££–£££**

St Agnes
Driftwood Spars Hotel, Trevaunance Cove, tel: 01872-552428, fax: 01872-553701; www.driftwoodspars.com En suite rooms, some with sea views, in 17th-century inn beside the bay. **£–££**

St Germans
Buttervilla Farm, Polbathic, Torpoint, tel: 01503-230315; www.butttervilla.com A lovely renovated farmhouse in 15 acres (6 hectares) of open countryside, close to the sea. **££**

St Ives
Blue Hayes, Trelyon Avenue, tel: 01736-797129; www.bluehayes.co.uk Set above Porthminster Beach this recently renovated hotel is tastefully furnished and comfortable. **££–£££**
Carbis Bay Hotel, Carbis Bay, tel: 01736-795311; www.carbisbayhotel.co.uk Set in large grounds overlooking a spectacular beach. Heated outdoor pool. Restaurant has AA rosette. **£££**
Garrack Hotel, Burthallan Lane, tel: 01736-796199; www.garrack.com On a hill near the Tate; large garden overlooking Porthmeor Beach. Indoor spa pool. Family run. **£££**

St Keyne
Well House, 3 miles (5 km) south of Liskeard, tel: 01579-342001, fax: 01579-343891; www.wellhouse.co.uk Croquet on the lawn, outdoor pool, tennis. First-rate restaurant offering local specialities. Winner of the *Good Hotel Guide* César award in 2004. **££–£££**

Sennen Cove
The Old Success, tel: 01736-871232, fax: 01736-871457; www.oldsuccess.com

B&B with the NT
More than 80 tenants of National Trust properties offer bed and breakfast accommodation. Most of it is fairly inexpensive and invariably the properties are attractive ones, set in beautiful countryside. Contact the NT on tel: 0870-458 4000 for a copy of their leaflet giving full details.

Friendly old inn right by the sea, with fantastic views. Excellent off-season special breaks. **££**

Tintagel
Bossiney House Hotel, tel: 01840-770240, fax: 01840-770501; www.bossineyhouse.co.uk Great views, heated indoor pool and a respected restaurant; ½ mile from village. **££**

Truro
The Hundred House Hotel, Ruan Highlanes, Roseland Peninsula, nr Truro, tel: 01872-501336; www.hundredhousehotel.co.uk A 19th-century house in 3 acres (1.2 hectares). The Fish in the Fountain restaurant is excellent. Good special breaks. **££**
The Royal, Lemon Street, tel: 01872-270345; www.royalhotelcornwall.co.uk Modern decor in a traditional Georgian building. Comfortable and central. **££**

Isles of Scilly
Harbourside Hotel, St Mary's, tel: 01720-422352; e-mail: mail@harbourside1.freeserve.co.uk On the quay, near sandy beaches. Fishing, bike hire, free golf; taxi service to/from heliport. **££**
Hell Bay Hotel, Bryher, tel: 01720-422947; e-mail: hellbay@aol.com A stylish hotel; beautiful gardens and fine views. Children's playroom. **££**
New Inn, Tresco, tel: 01720-422844; e-mail: newinn@tresco.co.uk Near New Grimsby waterfront. Collects guests from quay/heliport. Heated pool. **££**

INDEX

Accommodation **94**
Active Holidays ..**88**
Antony House **22, 80**
Architecture and Design **79**
Arthur, King **7, 10–11, 14, 72–3**
Barbara Hepworth Museum...........**59**
Betjeman, John ..**32, 70, 81**
Bodmin **29**
Bodmin Moor **29**
Boscastle **74**
Botallack **53**
Blisland **32**
Bolventor **32**
Bryher, Isles of Scilly **56**
Bude **75**
Cadgwith **44**
Caerhys Castle ...**80**
Calstock **19**
Camborne ...**61–62**
Camelford **72**
Cape Cornwall ...**53**
Castle Dore **28**
Cawsand **22**
Charlestown.......**34**
Chysauster **10**
Climate **12**
Coombe **75**
Cotehele House....**8, 19, 21, 79**
Coverack **44**
Culdrose.............**45**
Devoran **39**
Dozmary Pool **32**
Du Maurier, Daphne **26, 28, 32, 44, 80**
Durgan **43**
Eden Project .. **33–4**
Egloshayle **70**
Environment **12–13**
Falmouth **39**
Festivals.............**82**
Food and Drink ..**85**
Fowey **26–7**
Geology...............**8**
Glendurgan Gardens **42–3**

Godolphin House **46**
Golitha Falls **32**
Goonhilly Earth Station **44**
Graham, Winston **46, 81**
Gunnislake.........**20**
Gwithian **60**
Hawker, Robert Stephen **69, 75, 81, 83**
Hardy, Thomas ..**69, 74, 80**
Hayle **60**
Helford...............**44**
Heligan Gardens **35**
Helston...............**46**
Hepworth, Barbara **59–60, 77, 78**
History **14–15**
Isles of Scilly **54**
Jamaica Inn ..**26, 32**
Kingsand **22**
Kynance **45**
Lamorna Cove ...**45**
Lamorna Valley ..**51**
Land's End **52–3**
Language **11–2**
Lanhydrock **31**
Launceston..........**20**
Launceston Steam Railway **21**
Lelant **60**
Liskeard **23**
Literary Cornwall **80**
Little Petherick ..**69**
Lizard................**44**
Long Cross Victorian Garden **71**
Looe.................**24–5**
Lost Gardens of Heligan **35**
Lostwithiel.........**28**
Malpas **37**
Marazion **50**
Mary Newman's Cottage **18**
Mawgan **43**
Mawgan Porth ...**66**
Menabilly...........**28**
Mevagissey **35**
Millbrook...........**22**

Minack Theatre ..**52**
Morvah **52**
Morwenstow **75**
Mount Edgcumbe House **22**
Mousehole **51**
Mulfra Quoit **9**
Mullion **45**
Mylor **39**
National Maritime Museum...........**41**
National Seal Sanctuary..........**43**
Newlyn **50, 77**
Newlyn Gallery **15, 50, 77**
Newquay **64–5**
Nicholson, Ben ..**58, 59, 78**
Opie, John **63, 77**
Padstow **67–8**
Painting and Sculpture **77**
Par **33**
Paradise Park **60, 93**
Pendennis Castle **40**
Penwith **50**
Penzance **47–9**
Perranporth **64**
Perran Sands **64**
Polperro **25**
Polridmouth Cove **27**
Polruan...............**26**
Pool **62**
Port Isaac **71**
Portloe...............**37**
Port Navas **43**
Port Quin **70**
Portreath **62–3**
Practical Information **90**
Prideaux Place, Padstow **68**
Quiller-Couch, Arthur **81**
Readymoney Cove **27**
Redruth **62**
Restormel Castle **28**
Roseland Peninsula **37**

Saltash **18**
St Agnes **63**
St Agnes, Isles of Scilly **57**
St Cleer **32, 79**
St Columb Major **66**
St Enedoc church**70**
St Germans ..**21, 79**
St Ives **58–60**
St Just **53**
St Keyne's Well ..**24**
St Helen's, Isles of Scilly **56**
St Mary's, Isles of Scilly **55**
St Martin's, Isles of Scilly **57**
St Mawes **38–9**
St Mawgan..........**66**
St Michael's Mount **49**
St Neot................**31**
Sennen **53**
Slaughterbridge ..**72**
Stratton..............**75**
Tate St Ives **59***
Tean, Isles of Scilly **56**
Tintagel **73–4**
Trebah **43**
Tregony **37**
Trelissick Gardens **38–9**
Trelowarren **44**
Trematon Castle **21**
Trenance **65**
Trengwainton......**50**
Trerice **65**
Tresco, Isles of Scilly **56**
Trevarno Garden **46**
Trevenaunce Cove **63**
Trewithen...........**38**
Truro **36–7**
Veryan **37**
Wadebridge.......**69**
Wallis, Alfred ...**51, 58, 59, 78**
Wendron **46**
Zennor Quoit **9**
Zennor **53**